Hg2|Sydney

A Hedonist's guide to Sydney

Written by Michelle Wranik

PUBLISHER – Tremayne Carew Pole
EDITING – Nick Clarke
DESIGN – Nick Randall
MARKETING – Marilyn McDonald
MAPS – Richard Hale & Nick Randall
REPRO – Advantage Digital Print
PUBLISHER – Filmer Ltd
PHOTOGRAPHS –
Danks Street Depot © Some rights reserved by Allerina & Glen MacLarty

Email – info@hg2.com
Website – www.hg2.com
Published in the United Kingdom in 2012 by
Filmer Ltd
10th Floor, Newcombe House,
45 Notting Hill Gate, London W11 3LQ

ISBN – 978-1-905428-63-2

Hg2|Sydney

How to…

A Hedonist's guide to Sydney is broken down into easy-to-use sections: Sleep, Eat, Drink, Snack, Party, Culture, Shop, Play and Info. In each section you'll find detailed reviews and photographs. At the front of the book is an introduction to Sydney and an overview map, followed by introductions to the main areas and more detailed maps. On each of these maps, the places we have featured are laid out by section, highlighted on the map with a symbol and a number. To find out about a particular place simply turn to the relevant section, where all entries are listed alphabetically. Alternatively, browse through a specific section (e.g. Eat) until you find a restaurant you like the look of. Surrounding your choice will be a coloured box – each colour refers to a particular area of the Sydney. Simply turn to the relevant map to find the location.

Book your hotel on Hg2.com

We believe that the key to a great Sydney break is choosing the right hotel. Our unique site now enables you to browse through our selection of hotels, using the interactive maps to give you a good feel for the area as well as the nearby restaurants, bars, sights, etc., before you book. Hg2 has formed partnerships with the hotels featured in our guide to bring them to readers at the lowest possible price. Our site now incorporates special offers from selected hotels, as well information on new openings.

The concept

Ever had the feeling, when in an exciting new city, that its excitements were eluding you? That its promise failed to be delivered because you lacked the keys to unlock it? That was exactly what happened to Hg2's founder, Tremayne Carew Pole, who, despite landing in Budapest equipped with all the big-name travel guides, ended up in a turgidly solemn restaurant when all he wanted was a cool locals' hangout. After a wasted weekend, he quit his job and moved to Prague to write the first Hg2 guide. That was back in 2004, and since then, Hg2 has gone on to publish 32 city guides globally, all with the same aim in mind: to offer independent, insiders' advice to intelligent, urbane travellers with a taste for fine design, good food, the perfect Martini, and a city's inside track. Our take on hedonism is not just about pedal-to-the-metal partying, but a respect for the finer things in life.

Unlike many other guidebooks, we pride ourselves on our independence and integrity. We eat in all the restaurants, drink in all the bars, and go wild in all the nightclubs – all totally incognito. We charge no-one for the privilege of appearing in the guide, refuse print advertising, and include every place at our own discretion. With teams of knowing, on-the-ground contacts, we cover all the scenes but the tourist trap scene – from the establishment to the underground, from bohemia to the plutocrats' playgrounds, from fetish to fashiony drag, and all the places between and beyond, including the commercial fun factories and the neighbourhood institutions. We then present our findings in a clean, logical layout and a photograph accompanying every review, to make your decision process a quick, and effective one, so you can just get amongst what suits you best. Even the books' design is discreet, so as to avoid the dreaded 'hapless tourist' look.

Updates

Hg2 has developed a network of journalists in each city to review the best new hotels, restaurants, bars, clubs, etc, and to keep track of the latest openings. To access our free updates as well as the digital content of each guide, simply log onto our website www.Hg2.com and register. We welcome your help. If you have any comments or recommendations, please feel free to email us at info@hg2.com.

Michelle Wranik

Michelle is a Sydney-based writer and editor who ditched a career as a news journalist to write about the finer things in life; namely travel, food and booze. Her love of exploration has taken her across the globe, with stints living in Japan, London and most recently Dubai, where she edited Time Out's stable of travel magazines. Michelle returned home to Sydney in 2009 where freelance work for publications like the Sydney Morning Herald, the Boston Globe, CNN Traveller, the Daily Telegraph, GQ and Cosmopolitan, along with a regular newspaper column about her urban escapades helps to fund her travel and cocktail habit. Michelle loves gin & tonics and expertly made Negronis, the Omani desert, palm trees, bossa nova, and summer days absorbing sun, salt and sand at Sydney beaches. She doesn't loathe much, but egg white omelettes really get her goat. ("What have you people got against yolk?"). What makes her a hedonist? "My mantra. One negroni, two negroni, three negroni, floor."

■ Sydney

Sydney is a shameless flirt. She beckons and sashays with a harbour that never fails to impress, and beaches that rate among the world's finest. She winks seductively with chic waterfront restaurants, where you can order a dozen oysters and French Champagne at midday and toast a faultless summer's day. She knows she is, in the words of Derek Zoolander, ridiculously good-looking and her proud, if not smug, inhabitants know it, too.

Aside from being blessed with remarkable natural beauty, it's not difficult to see why Sydney consistently rates highly among the world's most liveable cities. Surf beaches, a healthy outdoor lifestyle and a sun-kissed Aussie summer are just some of the drawcards. Add to that a flamboyant gay and lesbian community, a cutting-edge culinary scene and a vibrant nightlife, and the picture becomes even prettier. Even in winter the temperature can hover around 15-20 degrees celsius.

Geographically, Sydney is one of the world's largest cities and it has a tendency to sprawl rather than scale heights, stretching from the golden sands of Bondi Beach to the misty Blue Mountain ranges and Hunter Valley wine region. Within its urban reaches, however, is where we've based this guide, and these days there's plenty to explore and absorb in the ever-evolving inner-city neighbourhoods. It may have done so in the past, but the city isn't relying on its sparkling harbour and string of beaches to pull the crowds anymore. Sydneysiders are also growing up – maturing and fine-tuning increasingly discerning tastes and demands for fashion-forward boutiques, gourmet food and edgy bars. There will always be beer, barbecues and the beach, of course, but these days a local is far more enamoured with what's unique, specialised and bespoke – say, an Argentinean steakhouse, an absinthe bar or a boutique selling custom-made Japanese sneakers.

Culturally, Sydneysiders are multi-ethnic, diverse and impossible to categorise. A quick 10-minute stroll through the city's streets might yield a mix of well-heeled city workers, hipsters and willowy fashionistas, to a dreadlocked surfer, a group of Asian university students or an Indian businessman – if not all on the same block. But you can forget what you've heard about the laid-back, lazy Australian, because locals have a work-hard, party-harder attitude, and keeping up with a bar-hopping Sydneysider can take a liver of steel. Come the weekend, however – especially during a sunny summer's day – and locals from all walks of life slow the pace right down, relaxing with a dip at the beach, a picnic at a harbourside park or over a schooner at the beating heart of any Australian city – the pub.

Sydney

SLEEP

1. Barrenjoey House
2. Bells @ Kincare
3. Cockatoo Island
4. Jonas Whale Beach
5. Pacific Road House
6. Pretty Beach House

EAT

7. Ad Lib
8. Jonas Whale Beach
9. Pilu

SNACK

10. Allpress Roastery Café
11. Barrenjoey House
12. Boat House Palm Beach
13. Brasserie Bread Bakery Café
14. Bronte Road Bistro
15. Nielsen Park Café Kiosk

PARTY

16. Enmore Theatre

CULTURE

17. 2 Danks Street

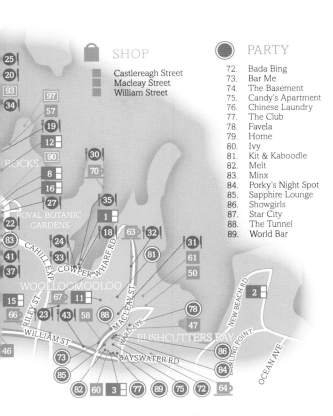

SHOP

Castlereagh Street
Macleay Street
William Street

PARTY

72. Bada Bing
73. Bar Me
74. The Basement
75. Candy's Apartment
76. Chinese Laundry
77. The Club
78. Favela
79. Home
80. Ivy
81. Kit & Kaboodle
82. Melt
83. Minx
84. Porky's Night Spot
85. Sapphire Lounge
86. Showgirls
87. Star City
88. The Tunnel
89. World Bar

SNACK

63. Bottega del Vino
64. Café Hernandez
65. Café Sopra
66. Detour Espresso Bar
67. Harry's Café de Wheels
68. Little Ethels
69. Plan B
70. Poolside Café
71. Le Renaissance Cafe Pattisserie

CULTURE

90. Art Gallery of N.S.W.
91. Bangarra Dance Theatre
92. Lyric Theatre
93. M.C.A.
94. State Theatre
95. Sydney Theatre
96. Sydney Dance Company
97. Sydney Opera House
98. Theatre Royal

CBD & Inner City (South)

◧ SLEEP

1. Fraser Suites
2. Kirketon
3. Medusa

◉ EAT

4. A Tavola
5. Bentley Bar
6. Berta
7. Boca
8. Bodega
9. Buzo Trattoria
10. The Commons
11. Din Tai Fung
12. Duke Bistro
13. Four in Hand
14. Golden Century
15. Hugos Bar Pizza
16. Longrain
17. Marque
18. Monkey Magic
19. Pizza E Birra
20. Porteno
21. Spice I Am
22. Table for 20
23. Tetsuya
24. Toko

■ DRINK

25. Absinthe Salon
26. Café Pacifico
27. The Commons Local
    Eating House & Bar
28. Doctor Pong
29. Eau de Vie
30. Fico
31. Flinders Hotel
32. Hunky Dory Social Club
33. Lo-Fi
34. The Lord Dudley
35. Love Tilly Devine
36. Madame Fling Flong
37. Mille Vini
38. Pocket Bar
39. Shady Pines Saloon
40. Sticky
41. Tokonoma Shochu Bar & Lounge
42. Victoria Room
43. Wine Library

■ Eastern Suburbs

Hip, affluent, and both glitzy and gritty, the Eastern Suburbs is a contradictory collective of some of the most intriguing Sydney suburbs, stretching from the eastern part of the city centre all the way to the world-famous sands of Bondi Beach. Darlinghurst and Surry Hills are two of the most bohemian areas; each a thriving foodie haven where streets and laneways are filled with young blood cafés like Forbes & Burton or Four Ate Five, fashionable restaurants like Toko or Marque, and edgy bars –head for Shady Pines Saloon for whisky, Sticky for cocktails and Flinders Hotel for beer. Much of the action is concentrated along Crown Street, known for its kitsch vintage boutiques, trendy eateries and ever-present slew of carefully dishevelled hipsters riding fixie bicycles. Along Oxford Street, globally renowned for the annual Gay & Lesbian Mardi Gras parade, you will find the flamboyant heart of Sydney's large gay community, along with lively gay bars and nightclubs, mostly concentrated around Taylors Square. A short walk away, the length of Victoria Street in Darlinghurst is crammed with some of Sydney's oldest cafés and cosy eateries. Tropicana Caffe and Bar Coluzzi are the most famous. This strip is particularly buzzy in the evening, making it an atmospheric spot to grab a quick meal before toying with the madness of the city's red light district Kings Cross or "The Cross," as it's affectionately known. While it's not nearly as naughty as it once was, a good measure of hanky panky continues to coexist alongside a thriving mishmash of nightclubs, bars and strip clubs. Stroll along the main drag of Darlinghurst Road to get an eyeful of burly bouncers and riff-raff aplenty. Around the corner, the tree-lined residential streets and Art Deco buildings of Potts Point are less frenetic, with a number of stylish eateries and boutiques.

Further east towards Bondi, you will smell the money far before you spot the Bentleys in Darling Point, Rushcutters Bay, Double Bay, Rose Bay and Woollahra. These wealthy, fashionable suburbs are characterised by leafy streets, waterfront parks with sailing clubs, beautifully maintained Victorian terrace houses, sprawling harbourfront penthouses, galleries, high-end fashion boutiques and upmarket eateries like Buzo and Bistro Moncur. The epicentre is chic Paddington, the city's upscale shopping precinct where eastern suburbs princesses flex their credit cards at boutiques stocking only the most fashion-forward Australian labels. Most are clustered along Glenmore Road and Oxford Street.

Towards the coast, the eastern suburbs culminate at Bondi Beach, Australia's most famous strip of sand – home to backpackers, surfers, perma-tanned old-timers and a hub of pubs and barefoot eateries selling salads, chai tea and fresh fruit juice. The area around North Bondi is preferred by local hipsters, who schlep around in

cut-off Ksubi jeans and designer sunglasses. They congregate on the so-called 'Grassy Knoll', a small park overlooking the north end of the beach, or at North Bondi Italian Food, which can be unbearably rife with poseurs at times. At the south end of the beach, pass toned, taut locals practising yoga on the sand and head to Icebergs Bar & Restaurant. Strip off for a dip in the iconic ocean pool below, or stay dry upstairs sipping cocktails and enjoying the views with a crowd besieged by Sydney's most prolific scenesters and A-listers. Not a fan of rubber-necking and one-upmanship? Nothing quite beats stretching the legs and lungs along the famous Bondi-Bronte walk, which takes in cracking vistas of the ocean, all the way to Bronte Beach.

SLEEP

1. Hughenden
2. Ravesi's
3. Tivoli Villa

 EAT

4. Bistro Moncur
5. Corner House
6. Iceberg
7. North Bondi Italian Food

Eastern Suburbs

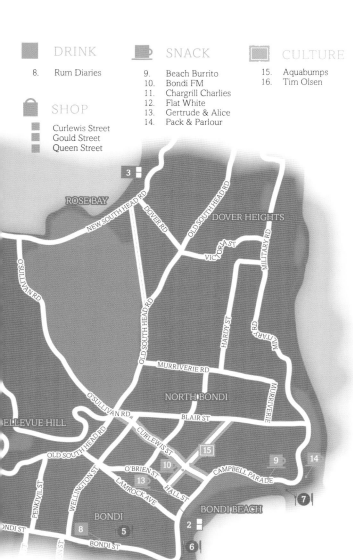

DRINK
8. Rum Diaries

SHOP
- Curlewis Street
- Gould Street
- Queen Street

SNACK
9. Beach Burrito
10. Bondi FM
11. Chargrill Charlies
12. Flat White
13. Gertrude & Alice
14. Pack & Parlour

CULTURE
15. Aquabumps
16. Tim Olsen

ROSE BAY

NEW SOUTH HEAD RD

DOVER RD

OLD SOUTH HEAD RD

DOVER HEIGHTS

VICTORIA ST

MILITARY RD

O'SULLIVAN RD

OLD SOUTH HEAD RD

HARDY ST

MILITARY RD

MURRIVERIE RD

NORTH BONDI

MURRIVERIE

O'SULLIVAN RD

BLAIR ST

BELLEVUE HILL

CURLEWIS ST

15

OLD SOUTH HEAD RD

O'BRIEN ST

10

CAMPBELL PARADE

9

14

PENKIVIL ST

WELLINGTON ST

13

HALL ST

LAMROCK AVE

7

BONDI BEACH

BONDI

8

5

2

BONDI ST

6

BONDI ST

Inner West

The Inner West of Sydney is a melting pot of ethnicities and eclectic subcultures and home to a diverse bunch of Sydneysiders, from university students and hippies to well-heeled thespians and young DINKYs buying their first property.

West of the city centre and only a short ferry ride from Circular Quay, Balmain was once a working-class suburb with a knockabout pub on every corner. Today, it's a wealthy part of Sydney, famous for its classic Australian pubs like The London, friendly village atmosphere and a perennially buzzy café strip along Darling Street. It has a tendency to become particularly crammed with breakfasting locals during the weekends – you can scarcely walk two metres before bumping into pram-pushing yummy mummies or becoming tangled in a dog leash. It's the same story if you continue along Darling Street west towards Rozelle, a suburb renowned for its cluster of charity op-shops, second-hand stores and Saturday thrift markets.

Closer to the city outskirts, it's a similar atmosphere over in quirky Glebe, well loved for its slew of ethnic eateries, bookstores and outdoor vintage markets, held every Saturday in the public school on Glebe Point Road (see Shop). Just across Parramatta Road and the green expanse of Victoria Park is the start of the anything-goes suburb of Newtown, the favourite precinct for lesbians, Goths and myriad offbeat subcultures. Stroll along the car-clogged King Street to explore vintage clothing boutiques, second-hand book stores, dive pubs and it seems, more Thai restaurants than Bangkok itself.

Nearer to the CBD, the former industrial areas of Chippendale and Darlington have quietly morphed into a stomping ground for Sydney's noveaux hipsters. Once a derelict zone filled with factories and commercial buildings, it's one of Sydney's

most up-and-coming urban precincts, awash with stylish warehouse apartment conversions, hip eateries like Café Giulia (see Eat) and independent art galleries like White Rabbit (see Culture). There's a hint of New York City attitude among the area's eclectic inner-city dwelling residents, who are working independently to create community grocery stores and pocket gardens in otherwise gritty, urban surrounds.

Redfern is another former working-class suburb shaking off its bad reputation, mostly caused by social unrest surrounding poorer Aboriginal communities and a high concentration of housing commission apartments. Both Redfern and nearby Waterloo aren't the rough part of town anymore, having been steadily gentrified with swanky residential developments, art galleries and trendy restaurants and cafés opening nearly every month. Danks Street in Waterloo is the best example – particularly 2 Danks Street with its ten galleries (see Culture) and adjacent Danks Street Depot café. Also worth a look is CarriageWorks, a multi-purpose arts venue injecting an immense amount of cultural vibrancy into a former railway yard. Tell a Sydneysider you've explored these cool-kid precincts, and you'll instantly earn street cred.

Inner West

 EAT

1. Bloodwood
2. La Boheme
3. Efendy
4. Riverview Hotel & Dining
5. Rosso Pomodoro

 DRINK

6. The London
7. Welcome Hotel

 SNACK

8. About Life
9. Bertoni Cassalinga
10. Black Star
11. Deus ex Machine
12. The Little Marionette
13. Shortlist
14. Toby's Estate

 PARTY

15. The Vanguard

 CULTURE

16. Carriage Works
17. At Perry Lane
18. Kate Owen Gallery

25

North Shore & Northern Beaches

The leafy, wealthy North Shore is characterised by conservative private schools, multi-million dollar mansions and magnificent surf beaches – including Palm Beach, where Aussie soap Home & Away is filmed. The North Shore begins at Kirribilli, the harbour-front area around the north pylon of the Harbour Bridge, though Sydneysiders call anything north of the harbour 'north of the bridge'. Stop here for laps under the bridge at the Olympic-sized, outdoor North Sydney Pool, or a meander around the monthly Kirribilli markets, adored by Sydney fashionistas. Skip Luna Park, an amusement park made up of sorry rollercoasters and garish rides – it's the bane of existence for wealthy locals who have long complained about the noise. Further north, the highbrow suburb of Mosman is worthy of exploration, at least to gaze longingly at the homes of Sydney's highest income earners. Many of these sprawling, modern mansions overlook the gorgeous vistas of Sydney harbour out to north head – but even plebeians can enjoy the same view at Taronga Zoo, which straddles the harbourfront. Nearby, a bushland walkway with tremendous harbour views leads all the way to Balmoral Beach, one of the city's prettiest habour beaches.

Further north, and only a 15-30 minute ferry ride from Circular Quay, Manly is famous for its surf beach. The area was once stereotyped as a haven for rowdy, drunken brawls but over the past few years the police have waged war on wayward pubs, enforcing earlier closing hours. Alight at the ferry terminal, perpetually abuzz with eateries and bars like Hugos Bar Pizza Manly and the Manly Wharf Hotel, particularly crammed with drinkers on a hot, summer's afternoon. The corso area towards the beach also teems with brozed locals; it's tacky in a beachy way, littered with ice-creameries, burger joints and surf stores selling colourful bikinis and board shorts. Make sure to explore the peaceful, wave-less Shelley Beach at the south end – popular with scuba divers and snorkellers – and the numerous harbour beaches. Some are only accessible by kayak, hidden in the bushy headland along North Head.

It's a great idea to rent a car and explore the northern beaches to soak up that quintessentially laid-back, Aussie beach lifestyle. From Manly, there is another 20-kilometres of beaches to explore like Collaroy, Longreef, Dee Why and Narrabeen, all popular with serious surfers. Each beach is vastly different, but most have their own surf club and kiosk – a basic cafeteria selling soft drinks, pies and sandwiches. Some have a bustling village a few sandy footsteps away, with an excellent array of cafés, pharmacies, pubs and shops overflowing with suncream, sarongs and sunglasses. The farthest beaches take at least an hour's drive from the city, and are the wealthiest spots – particularly Whale Beach, where singer George Michael recently purchased a property. The glorious Palm Beach – Sydney's version of The Hamptons – ends in a peninsula, with a magnificent surf beach on one side and peaceful river on the other side, divided by a native bush headland topped by the Barrenjoey Lighthouse. Many upper-crust Sydneysiders are lucky enough to have a holiday house here – visiting most weekends to escape the rat race.

North Shore

 SLEEP

1. Quarantine Station

 EAT

2. Bathers Pavilion
3. Hugos Bar Pizza
4. Manly Pavilion
5. Neutral Bay Bar & Dining Room
6. Public Dining Room

SNACK

7. Bean Drinking
8. Burnt Orange
9. Olio Mediterranean Brasserie
10. Ripples

 PARTY

11. Greenwood Hotel

Tivolli Villa

sleep…

In a city that totes its harbour as proudly as a socialite totes her Birkin handbag, the impressive water views from many of Sydney's five-star hotels means all too many have rested on their laurels in the style and design departments. After all, who's admiring the mahogany and full-grain Italian leather chaise lounge when there's a postcard-perfect view of yachts beneath the Harbour Bridge from the window? Some of the big hotel groups are well aware it takes more than a gorgeous view to get a hedonist into bed. The Shangri-La is a case example of a Sydney hotel upping the ante. It already had a trifecta of heartstopping views, one-hatted restaurant and a stylish cocktail bar, yet it forged ahead to launch Chi The Spa in 2010, a globally-renowned Asian spa with world-class pampering treatments. Another behemoth hotel to watch is Star City, a casino and five-star hotel that is taking a gamble on seducing the travelling gourmand. The hotel is planning a total of seven restaurants as part of its current multimillion-dollar refurbishment, including a new venue set up by chef David Chang of Momofuku fame. Oh, happy days.

Bedding down around the harbour offers an obvious drawcard and easy access to the big five: the Opera House, the Harbour Bridge, the Botanic Gardens, CBD shopping and the Circular Quay ferry terminal. But you're on holiday remember, and there are several dozen beaches to explore, so we've taken the liberty of including a couple of dreamy beachside properties – both private rentals and charming homestyle B&Bs, where you can roll from bed to sand within minutes and become reacquainted with that long-lost feeling: relaxation. Jonah's at Whale Beach has it down to an art form, with luxury to boot – it's the only Relais & Châteaux-rated hotel in Australia with Mykonos-style views over the ocean and an attached namesake restaurant that's worth the trip alone.

Equally luxurious weekend beach escapes in quintessential Australian bushland surrounds can be found at Pretty Beach House and at Bells at Killcare, two weekender hotspots that afford a glimpse into the charmed lives of Sydney's wealthier social circles.

For the urbanite who can't get enough of the city buzz, there are a handful of boutique hotels in the inner city, though Sydney has a lamentable shortage. The fashionable Establishment, Medusa and Kirketon, however, are consistently popular and all three will appeal to the designphile, with chic, minimalistic-cool interiors. The latter two are in Darlinghurst, an edgy area with Sydney's hippest bars, restaurants and nightclubs – take that as gospel.

You've travelled across continents and oceans to get here and jet-lag is a bitch. So we're guessing many of you want to stay a little bit longer. On that note, we've included a few select apartment stays like Potts Point View, Darling Point Pad, Fraser Suites and Quay Grand Suites, where washing machines and slick, modern kitchens make your trip just that little bit more comfortable.

the best hotels…

Our favourites:
Establishment
Jonah's Whale Beach
Kirketon
Pacific Road House
Park Hyatt
Potts Point View
Pretty Beach House
Ravesi's
Shangri-La
Tivoli Villa

For Style:
Establishment
Kirketon
Pacific Road House
Pretty Beach House
Tivoli Villa

For Atmosphere:
Darling Point Pad
Potts Point View
Pretty Beach House
Shangri-La
Tivoli Villa

For Location:
Blue
Darling Point Pad
Jonah's Whale Beach
Park Hyatt
Ravesi's

Barrenjoey House (left)

1108 Barrenjoey Road, Palm Beach (opposite Palm Beach Wharf)
Tel: 02 9974 4001
www.barrenjoeyhouse.com.au
Rates: AU$180–AU$220

Set on the tranquil Pittwater side of Palm Beach, Barrenjoey House is a coastal boutique beach house above its namesake restaurant, across from the Pittwater riverfront with its Norfolk pines and ferries chugging in the distance. Don't come here expecting Belgian chocolates on your pillow, but rest assured the understated Australian charm will win you over. A guesthouse since 1923, it has three en-suite rooms and four with shared bathrooms, and while there's nothing luxurious about either, most have water glimpses and all are styled in comfy, appealing beach house décor, with seashells, soft linen, hardwood floors, wicker furniture and native Natural Essence bath products. Best bring a book or hone your conversation skills because neither guest room has a television; there is a communal LCD television in the adjacent lounge room, equipped with a huge sofa and paintings of Polynesian natives adorning the walls. It's here where the managers sneak in early in the morning to drop off a help-yourself breakfast hamper for guests – think organic muesli, fresh tropical fruit, yoghurt, teas, coffee and sourdough. After exploring the area's beaches, there's little else to do except relax – curl up on the large sofa, or head downstairs to the restaurant, which happens to be one of the most popular on the northern beaches.

Style 6, Atmosphere 7, Location 9

Bells @ Killcare *(right)*
107 The Scenic Road,
Killcare Beach
Tel: 02 4360 2411
www.bellsatkillcare.com.au
Rates: from AU$350–500 including
gourmet breakfast hamper.

Nestled in beautifully landscaped gardens and bushland, Bells is chic, coastal retreat around an hour or so from Sydney (or 20 minutes by ferry from Palm Beach), otherwise known as rancho relaxo for well-heeled city slickers. The mix of two-storey and single-storey cottages are set around the main European-style manor house, which houses an award-winning restaurant headed by chef Stefano Manfredi. The cottages are ideal for couples in search of privacy, peace and quiet, with private entries, timber-decked bal-

conies, plantation shutters and striking blue-and-white striped cushions. All are equipped with the necessary comforts like supersoft king-sized beds, spa baths and Aveda products, and each cottage comes with a gourmet hamper packed with bacon, eggs, organic muesli and bread, so you can cook breakfast at your leisure. Settle in with a good book on the balcony, or wander through the gardens, which feature fishponds, wildflowers and manicured lawns. There are around seven beaches and national parks to explore a short drive away, and if you need some inspiration, the warm, chatty proprietors Brian and Karina Barry are happy to share their local knowledge. Otherwise, stay put on the premises – cooling off in a swimming pool or indulging in an Aboriginal-inspired massage or facial

at the Day Spa, set in a converted two-levelled barn.

Style 8, Atmosphere 8, Location 8

....

Blue *(top)*
The Wharf at Woolloomooloo, 6 Cowper Wharf Road, Woolloomooloo
Tel: 02 9331 9000
www.tajhotels.com
Rates: AU$250–300

Formerly the W Hotel, the 100-room Blue hotel is set on the Finger Wharf marina, home to a clutch of the city's most prestigious waterfront restaurants and within an extraordinary, historic wharf building that once functioned as a wool- and cargo-handling facility. Much of the building's original features have been preserved, like sweeping high ceilings, exposed timber and iron beams and rusty mechanical ramps, and the space has been subdivided between the hip hotel and luxurious apartments – many of which are owned by Sydney glitterati, namely Russell Crowe. The rooms run along each side of the hotel, while the super-sized central warehouse space in the centre houses Water Bar, a sexy cocktail bar with Swarovski crystal curtains. The best rooms face west, overlooking the wharf and Sydney city skyline. All are beautifully-appointed, with 250 thread-count cotton sheets, roomy bathrooms with Serendipity products, and chocolate-coloured hardwood furniture offset by blue tones and black-and-white photography. W Hotel regulars will notice some of the chain's elements remain; the gym is called Sweat, and among the M&Ms and Voss water, the in-room Munchie Boxes contain miniature bottles of flavoured Absolut vodka, Panadol and condoms. Blue's only downfall is the lack of discreet passage to the tiny indoor pool and gym. If you want to have a dip on a Saturday night, you'll have to stride past Water bar patrons in your swim gear.

Style 8, Atmosphere 7, Location 10

....

Cockatoo Island *(bottom)*
Cockatoo Island, Sydney Harbour
Tel: 02 8898 9774
www.cockatooisland.gov.au
Rates: AU$260–AU$780

Want to stay on an island, nearly all to yourself? Managed by the Sydney Harbour Federation Trust, Cockatoo Island is a ferry ride from Circular Quay. It already plays host to campers, music festivals and a seasonal cocktail bar – and fairly recently, the Federation-style buildings – which used to house convicts and misbehaved reformatory school girls – have been luxuriously refurbished into holiday accommodation. There are various styles to choose from, including one- and two-bedroom apartments and larger Federation houses that can sleep up to ten people. All have been beautifully restored with free-standing bathtubs, flatscreen televisions, CD and DVD players, iPod dock alarm clocks and board games. You need to bring all your food and booze across on the ferry, as the cottages are designed to be self-catering, but it's worth it. While all cottages feature modern kitchens equipped with basic utensils and washing machines, nothing beats cooking up a feast on the

barbecue on the outdoor terraces that face the city and Harbour Bridge.

Style 7, Atmosphere 7, Location 8

The Darling *(left)*
Point Pad
Darling Point, Sydney
Tel: 02 9331 2881
www.housesandapartments.com.au
Rates: from AU$800 (five-night minimum stay.)

Want to be the envy of all Sydneysiders? Then stay here. This glamorous, privately-rented penthouse apartment is the one we all dream of owning. Set high above Rushcutters Bay only minutes away from Potts Point cafés and the waterfront parklands below, this pimping pad spans the entire top floor of a stately 1930s mansion and has tear-inducing views of the shimmering harbour, yachts, ferries, the Harbour Bridge and more. The décor is exquisitely stylish, contemporary and hued in a brilliant white palette, and while there's a modern kitchen the two-bedroom property's period features are highlighted, particularly in the master bedroom, which features a beautiful French chandelier and a deep bathtub, and in the dining room and formal living room, which has a well-stocked library, a grand fireplace and ornate mirrors. However, most guests spend the majority of their time outside taking in the sensational harbour views on the gorgeous, sundrenched terrazzo, which opens out onto a lime-washed timber decked area with antique wooden daybeds, a six-seater dining table and a sexy hot tub. Did somebody say mojito?

Style 8, Atmosphere 9, Location 10

Diamant *(right)*
14 Kings Cross Road, Potts Point
Tel: 02 9295 8888
www.8hotels.com
Rates: from AU$150

For nocturnal mischief, the 77-room Diamant hotel couldn't be better situated. Downstairs, on the ground floor, there's the classy Time To Vino, a wine bar run by Clint Hillery, one of Sydney's most respected sommeliers. As for clubbers, you're less than two blocks away from the centre of the buzzy red light district of Kings Cross, home to the city's highest concentration of nightclubs. Design-wise, Diamant is sleek, chic and simple – it's a boutique hotel with a pared-back style; standard rooms are minimal and urban, with chocolate browns and caramel-coloured tones. Deluxe rooms are more spacious, and all rooms cover standard tech-needs with 42-inch plasma televisions and iPod docking stations. The Courtyard rooms have harbour glimpses and private, outdoor courtyards, but for those with cash to flash, try the penthouse suite, which has two balconies, a gourmet kitchen, a master bedroom with a pimping powder room, walk-in wardrobe and spa, and two guest rooms with en-suites. There's no gym on-site, though the concierge can supply you with free passes to Fitness First, located just a block away.

Style 7, Atmosphere 7, Location 9

Establishment *(left)*
5 Bridge Lane, CBD
Tel: 02 9240 3100
www.establishmenthotel.com
Rates: from AU$150

Easily one of Sydney's hippest addresses, every visiting celebrity, fashionista and designer worth their salt has shacked up in one of Establishment's minimalistic-cool suites, and the conglomerate of entertainment venues under one roof means there's little reason to venture elsewhere – it's all at your fingertips. Along with a stylish 31-room boutique hotel, you can sup cocktails in the moody Moroccan-styled Hemmesphere cocktail bar (see Drink) then dine on superb Japanese at Sushi-e or faultless cuisine at chef Peter Doyle's three-hatted est. restaurant (see Eat). To top it off, take the private elevator down to the VIP section of Tank nightclub (see Party) for a few hours of carousing – no 6am walk of shame required. Though the two penthouse suites require deep pockets, all other suites enjoy the same design aspects; think Bose sound systems, sumptuous king-sized beds and exposed wooden beams. You can even choose your room's colour scheme – slick dark or placid white. The bathrooms are equally stylistic, with tempered glass walls, marble vanities with Philippe Stark faucets, and perfectly placed Bvlgari products for a long, hot soak in the generously proportioned bathtub.

Style 9, Atmosphere 8, Location 9

Fraser Suites *(middle)*
488 Kent Street, Darling Harbour
Tel: 02 8823 8888
www.fraserhospitality.com
Rates: AU$222–473

This luxury, five-star serviced apartment hotel is such a well-hidden secret, the most savvy local wouldn't know it – even though it's directly opposite Tetsuya's (see Eat). Designed by architects Foster + Partners, the 42-level tower enjoys sweeping views over the city, the harbour and western Sydney. There are 201 luxurious studios, one- and two-bedroom suites,

and two plush duplex penthouses, and all manage to avoid that soulless atmosphere plaguing so many business hotels, with plump beds, flatscreen televisions and stylish décor in hues of gunmetal grey. Bonus points as it's one of the few hotels with windows that actually open. Those in the city for a longer stay will appreciate hidden washer/dryers and the stainless steel Schlott Seran kitchens, but take advantage of the location – along with Tetsuya's just across the road, the city's department stores and Chinatown eateries (we recommend Golden Century, see Eat) are only a leisurely stroll away. To burn off those pork buns, there's a well-equipped gymnasium, a spa and sauna, and a 20-metre indoor pool, cantilevered over Regent Place shopping precinct.

Style 7, Atmosphere 7, Location 8

Four Seasons *(right)*
Hotel Sydney
199 George Street, The Rocks
Tel: 02 9250 3100

www.fourseasons.com/sydney
Rate: from AU$275

The stately Four Seasons is a favourite with frequent travellers for exceptional service and classic, five-star comfort. The guest rooms have stunning harbour or city skyline views, 42-inch LCD televisions, DVD players and iPod/MP3 connectivity and all are stylishly equipped with solid Honduran mahogany furniture, rich silks and design lamps. The Italian marble bathrooms stock L'Occitane products while minibar trays are stuffed with treats like Jelly Belly jelly beans, Australian wine and vacuum-packed coffee and teas. For executive club members, swan up to level 32 for complimentary self-serve drinks and nibbles, but get there quick because there are only three water-view tables. There's a much classier ambience downstairs in the glamorous foyer, which tiers upwards to a sweeping staircase, complete with Art Deco chandeliers. On the mezzanine level, there's a serene spa, with beautifully-appointed separate men and women changing rooms, and six treatment rooms us-

ment rooms using Elemis and Sodashi products. It connects directly to the hotel's small outdoor pool, which, although a little dated, does wonders for a hangover.

Style 8, Atmosphere 8, Location 9

Grace Hotel *(left)*
77 York Street, corner
of King Street, CBD
Tel: 02 9272 6888
www.gracehotel.com.au
Rates: from AU$150

One of the city's best examples of prewar architecture, the Grace hotel was once an office block that was requisitioned during the Second World War for use as allied headquarters. It's since been refurbished, but the gorgeous Art Deco features, such as stained-glass insignias, ceiling lamps and terrazzo floors remain. Rooms are smart and hued with a tawny colour palette, hardwood writing desks and chenille sofas, along with king-sized beds with feather comforters and 32-inch flatscreen televisions. Not a fan of earthy tones? The hotel has a new concept called the 10 Rooms package, offering travellers the option of tailoring décor, style or even the colour scheme, with added luxuries depending on your mood – like an in-room espresso machine if you need an energy boost, or luxurious spa products if you need pampering. There's little else in the way of facilities, however, aside from the Grace Café downstairs which commands a people-watching corner post. Be warned; the hotel is perfectly placed for credit card destruction – it's only a few steps away from the city's department stores and the new Westfield shopping mall, and is dangerously close to King Street Wharf bars and restaurants. There's also a small arcade on the low

er ground floor with a beauty bar for eyebrow tidies and pedicures.

Style 7, Atmosphere 7, Location 9

 Hilton *(right)*
488 George Street, CBD
Tel: 02 9265 6045
www.hiltonsydney.com.au
Rates: from AU$300

Slick and contemporary, the Hilton earned its stripes very quickly since re-opening after a AU$145-million refurb, luring star chef Luke Mangan to head Glass Brassiere and leading mixologists to launch Zeta Bar (see Drink), an ode to the art of fine cocktails. With tongue-in-cheek accommodation packages like The Proposal, The Break-Up and The Provocateur – featuring an aphrodisiac-inspired degustation platter and saucy seduction tips from Sydney sex minx Madame Lash – the Hilton is a breath of fresh air in an otherwise dull five-star world. Entering through a light-filled glass lobby area with a 65-foot ceiling, check-in is swift and fuss-free. Rooms feature LCD televisions, black-out blinds (which help with light but not city noise), a pillow menu and must-pinch Crabtree and Evelyn La Source toiletries, while the hotel's Living Well fitness club has a 25-metre indoor swimming pool, cardiovascular gymnasium and free weights area. Along with standard suites, the hotel dips its toe into holistic realm with its Relaxation Suite and Room, which aims to create 'zones' to separate work, relaxation and indulgence, with partition doors, ergonomic work desks and chairs, and ultra-luxurious bathrooms.

Style 8, Atmosphere 8, Location 9

Hughenden *(left)*
14 Queen Street, Woollahra
Tel: 02 9363 4863
www.hughendenhotel.com.au
Rates: AU$150–388

A go-to for literary lovers or travellers wanting to stay somewhere that's more like a home, this stately Victorian mansion has worn many hats in its time. It was once home to Dr Frederick Harrison Quaife, who was a founding father of the British Medical Association and son of philosopher Barzillai Quaife. Then it became a Masonic Hall and a Ladies College before finally opening its doors in 1993 as a boutique hotel. There are 36 rooms and eight suites – including a few dog-friendly ones, and you can even stay in Dr Quaife's former room, which overlooks Queen Street. Its black marble fireplaces, oak furniture, grand staircase and even more grandiose Victorian-era rooms are well suited to the affluent area of Woollahra, which has leafy streets packed with galleries, million-dollar estates and high-end boutiques. Expect eccentrics discussing Dostoevsky in the Reading Room, high tea with fluffy scones and traditional teas and even jazz nights, where a pianist will tinkle the ivories of the baby grand piano in the lounge. The hotel's Quaifes Cafe and Restaurant serves a la carte dining, and there are plenty of top-notch restaurants and pubs situated along Queen Street and nearby Oxford Street.

Style 7, Atmosphere 8, Location 9

InterContinental *(right)*
117 Macquarie Street,
Circular Quay
Tel: 02 9253 9000
www.sydney.intercontinental.com
Rates: from AU$275

For seriously stupendous views of Sydney, book an executive room. The rooftop club lounge reserved exclusively for executive club guests has one of the most jawdropping vistas over Sydney harbour from an outdoor, wraparound decked balcony. Members often park themselves here from dawn and never leave – when you can have a deluxe breakfast and a macchiato on the terrace, nibble on scones and tea in the afternoon, and quaff a few cocktails at twilight, all for free, with free wireless internet, why would you? Throughout, the InterContinental epitomises five-star class. Built above the former Treasury, the lower level features heritage detailing like the restored sandstone façade and atrium ceiling above the Cortile Café, tasteful artworks (look out for a huge mural by Australian artist Tim Storrier) hung on the walls, and a Bose boutique in case you left your headphones at home. The hotel's 509 rooms and suites are generous, stylish and elegant, furnished with sizeable desks and sofas, elegant black-and-white-tiled bathrooms stocked with Elemis products and large windows. There are window seats (to gaze at the view while sipping a pinot) and thoughtful touches like double blinds so the blistering sunrise doesn't bust your beauty sleep – a godsend for the jet-lagged traveller.

Style 8, Atmosphere 8, Location 9

sleep...

Jonah's Whale Beach   *(top)*
69 Bynya Road, Whale Beach
Tel: 02 9974 5599
www.jonahs.com.au
Rates: from AU$529

A favourite weekend retreat for Sydney's glitziest and ritziest, Jonah's is a five-star boutique hotel perched atop the precipitous cliffs above Whale Beach, with heartstopping views over the Pacific Ocean. It's part of the Relais & Châteaux collection, an exclusive club of 480 of the world's most prestigious hotels, but the breezy atmosphere and welcoming smiles of Australian staffers give it such a relaxed vibe that it feels more like a luxury beach home. Each of the ten ocean retreat suites attached to the main house have balconies that open up onto incredible blue vistas of the ocean, but the best views are from the main terrazzo – the ultimate setting for a sunset martini. Guests requiring more privacy can hire out Jonah's Private, a separate property adjacent to the main retreat, which has three guest-rooms overlooking the pool. All rooms are stocked with essentials like an LCD television, iPod docking stereo and the obligatory slew of glossy travel magazines, while the limestone bathrooms are equipped with Bvlgari products, spas and rain showerheads. Rather than opulent luxury, the interiors are simple beach chic, with rattan sunloungers and framed seashells on the walls and crisp white linen – the perfect backdrop to sun-kissed skin. As for dining, guests are spoiled with Jonah's restaurant, with chef George Fransisco at the helm (see Eat). However, there's no problem with ordering in – the compendium lists local Thai and pizza joints, which you can have delivered to your room.

Style 8, Atmosphere 8, Location 10

Kirketon   *(bottom)*
229 Darlinghurst Road, Darlinghurst
Tel: 02 9332 2011
www.kirketon.com.au
Rates: from AU$145

Originally designed by Burley Katon Halliday, this 40-room boutique hotel was acquired by the Eight Hotels group in 2008, who commissioned designer Connie Alessi (Edge Design) to rework the interiors and conjure up something reminiscent of a Parisian boutique hotel (Costes, anyone?). Alessi chose moody boudoir chic for the hardwood hallways, which are painted a dramatic scarlet colour, while guest rooms are furnished simply with leather lounges, recurring tones of gunmetal grey, and black and silver gilded mirrors. Located a hop, skip and a stumble from the naughty red light playground of Sydney's King's Cross, the Kirketon will appeal to the night owls more than the throw-open-the-curtains-at-6am guest, and it's all too tempting to indulge in the area's chic restaurants, plentiful bars and nightclubs and need not fear dazzling sunlight and noise as all rooms have heavy drapes and double-glazed glass. If you're spending a night in, service is discreet, effortless and professional, with familial touches like DVDs to watch on LCD televisions and in-room dining available courtesy of the area's many restaurants. Passes to the Fitness First gymnasium down the

47

road come with the room – you might need them after a night guzzling cocktails at Eau de Vie, one of Sydney's hippest cocktail bars, located conveniently (or dangerously) just downstairs.

Style 9, Atmosphere 8, Location 9

Medusa *(top)*
267 Darlinghurst Road, Darlinghurst
Tel: 02 9331 1000
www.medusa.com.au
Rates: from AU$310

Near the mischievous red light district of Kings Cross, this grand, three-levelled terrace mansion is home to an elegant boutique hotel named after the beautiful yet terrifying mythical snake-haired maiden. Look out for the circular print of Carravaggio's Medusa, which hangs above the reception's marble mantlepiece in her honour. There are 18 rooms – the best are the oversized Grand rooms, featuring lofty ceilings, disused marble fireplaces with dramatic feature walls, along with designer chaise longues, suede and wood-panelled headboards, and Aveda toiletries. To the rear, the rooms overlook a central courtyard replete with trickling feature fountain and bamboo plants. Medusa's proximity to nightclubs, restaurants and Sydney's gay district make it ideal for the in-and-out traveller, and the hotel is fitted out accordingly – breakfast is only available by request, the compendium lists an exhaustive summary of the area's plentiful bars and restaurants and while there's a DVD library in the main room, the televisions are quite small. Other things to note: wireless internet is available for AU$5 per day, some rooms have kitchenettes, the hotel is dog-friendly and smoking isn't permitted – if you smoke, consider staying in the front Grand Room (which features a balcony) or one of the deluxe ground floor rooms, with courtyard access.

Style 9 Atmosphere 7 Location 9

Observatory *(bottom)*
89-113 Kent Street, CBD
Tel: 02 8248 5220
www.observatoryhotel.com.au
Rates: from AU$315

Resplendent with its brocade, gold gilt and 19th-century pomp, the Observatory has a luxuriously old-world style that will send minimalists running for the door. Part of the Orient-Express hotel chain, it's a five-star world of gleaming marble floors and columns, with over-stuffed chaise longues, polished armoires and heavy drapes filling every corner. Six of the executive suites are even named after the carriages on the legendary British Pullman passenger train; many of them with domed ceilings are flanked by traditional four-poster beds, and marble bathrooms stocked with Simplicity products. Despite its classic styling, the hotel mod-cons are all present and correct, with LCD televisions, DVD players and easily one of Sydney's most luxurious day spas (see Play). As for food and drinks, finicky gastronomes will quiver over the must-try seven-course degustation menu at Galileo restaurant, a Parisian-style bistro headed up by chef Masahiko Yomoda. After dinner, have a nightcap in either the Globe or Martini Bar – with all the antiques and novels

cramming mahogany shelves, it's like something plucked directly from Pride & Prejudice.

Style 8, Atmosphere 8, Location 8

Pacific Road House *(left)*
Pacific Road, Palm Beach
Tel: 02 9331 2881
www.beachouses.com.au
Rates: from AU$900

Set among the swaying eucalyptus trees and only a short stroll to the beach, this gorgeous, privately-rented mansion is the epitome of Australian beachside luxury and the huge north-easterly facing terrazzo will have you pinching your arm in disbelief. Overlooking the shimmering vista of Palm Beach and even the Barrenjoey Lighthouse in the distance, it's glamorous enough for a bikini model photoshoot and creates the perfect setting for a sunset Martini after a long, leisurely day at the beach. Overseen by Sydney design team Greg Natale Design, the interiors of this light-filled, 1950s house are a stylist's dream. Sleek white walls are offset by dark timber floors and breezy sheer curtains, with abstract artwork adorning the walls and plenty of sofas scattered throughout. With three spacious bedrooms and two bathrooms – each kitted out with a full range of superior linen, fresh towelling and Aveda toiletries – renting the house is a savvy choice for longer stays or those travelling in a group, with an open-plan main area made for entertaining. Cook up a feast in the modern, white gourmet kitchen, and dine either inside or out on the terrace. Either way, you won't want to leave in a hurry.

Style 10, Atmosphere 8, Location 9

Park Hyatt *(right)*
7 Hickson Road, The Rocks
Tel: 02 9256 1234
www.sydney.park.hyatt.com
Rates: from AU$695

Here is your box seat to one of the best harbour views in Sydney. Perched at the edge of water, nothing stands between the three-level Park Hyatt and its dress circle views of Sydney Harbour, though such billion-dollar real estate means guests pay through their teeth. When it comes to hospitality, however, the Park Hyatt is exemplary – butlers offer round-the-clock service and a full breakfast menu is served 24-hours a day. Rooms are strikingly modern with LCD televisions, DVD and CD players, black leather headboards, and lots of creamy leather and caramel tones, while the elegant bathrooms feature Italian marble in hues of grey and white, and are stocked with Italian Comfort Zone products. With 300-count linen and feather du-vets, the beds are superbly comfortable. Most rooms have balconies overlooking the harbour, while the Diplomatic suite has a choice of four private balconies, along with direct views of the Opera House – even from the spa bath. There are more views from the rooftop Iluka Spa, which uses an Australian organic skincare range, and more from the outdoor swimming pool. Try high tea at Harbour Kitchen & Bar, where you can nibble scones and sup tea or Nicolas Feuillatte Champagne while gazing at yet another postcard-perfect vista of the Opera House.

Style 8, Atmosphere 8, Location 10

51

Pretty Beach House *(left)*
83 Highview Road, Pretty Beach
Tel: 02 4360 1933
www.prettybeachhouse.com
Rates: from AU$1,700

Around 100-kilometres from Sydney on the Bouddi Peninsula, this private boutique retreat is set in tranquil native bushland and offers round-the-clock private butler service and a no-expenses-spared experience – whether you want to arrive by seaplane, helicopter (20 minutes from Sydney) or a skippered 40-foot yacht. The property sleeps a maximum of three couples in three villas, and there's a stunning main house that opens out to the communal swimming pool, where wooden carvings and artwork by prominent Australian artists like John Olsen and Arthur Boyd adorn the walls, along with an open log fireplace, a grand piano (a pianist can be arranged), a mezzanine bar and a well-stocked wine cellar. Award-winning Chef Stefano Manfredi serves light Mediterranean fare; guests usually dine communally in the main retreat, though dinner can be served anywhere – the grassed terraces, in your villa or even in the wine cellar, where a sommelier is at your service. Privacy is paramount and each villa features its own heated plunge pool, a decked terrace with a daybed, vintage leather armchairs, bathrooms equipped with rainshowers and locally-made Li'tya botanical products. Televisions are optional, though every room has a Bose SoundDock with iPod and wireless internet, along with Havaianas, and binoculars for spotting native wildlife. The beach is only a few minutes away through the bushland. While it's difficult to fault either of the villas, our money is on Treetops. It's adjacent to

the main house but offers slightly more privacy, is set over two levels and has a free-standing tub.

Style 10, Atmosphere 9, Location 8

Potts Point View *(right)*
Potts Point, Sydney
Tel: 02 9331 2881
www.housesandapartments.com.au
Rates: from AU$385

The ultimate urban pad, Potts Point View smacks of masculine sophistication. Grant Featherston of Artes Studio and Vico Magistretti for Cassina are the formidable design team behind the chic interiors of this oversized, one -bedroom apartment, with understated furnishings, sculptures and artwork scattered throughout. The icing on the cake is the apartment's glittering city skyline view, which takes in the Harbour Bridge, Opera House and CBD and looks particularly spectacular at night. With HD cable television, broadband internet and a sleek, all-marble bathroom, the apartment is beautifully equipped for those in Sydney on a longer stay, with Miele accessories and a gourmet kitchen. But those who want to make the most of the area's thriving dining scene only need stroll down the quiet cul-de-sac to reach the main streets, which are heaving with cafés, trendy eateries and bars. The nightclubs (and spicier joints of Kings Cross) are within walking distance, too.

Style 9, Atmosphere 8, Location 9

Quarantine Station *(left)*
North Head Scenic Drive, Manly
Tel: 02 9466 1551 / 02 9466 1500
www.qstation.com.au
Rates: from AU$205

One of Sydney's quirkier stays, but where else can you wake up to the sound of kookaburras, enjoy uninterrupted harbour views and spot native wildlife like fairy penguins and bandicoots meandering outside your suite? Five minutes from Manly or a short water taxi ride across the harbour, Q Station isn't as isolated as it was back in the 1800s, when the remote bushland cove quarantined migrant arrivals to thwart the spread of smallpox. Hundreds of hapless souls never made it out alive, and as a result, ghosthunters traipse through the site's former hospital each night on guided ghost tours. There are 72 boutique rooms,

but don't expect anything too snazzy. Stringent Australian heritage laws have heavily restricted renovation, meaning some suites don't have personal bathrooms. The first-class passenger rooms (ask for 25 or 27) do have private ensuites and French doors that open up to a communal verandah with million-dollar views of the harbour. From here, the resort's Engine Room bar and The Boilerhouse restaurant, which serves elegant cuisine, wine and artisanal Australian beers, are only a short stroll away. Considering the restrictions, rooms are decently kitted out; beds are super-soft, bathrooms are stocked with Romy products and there are LCD televisions, but some luxury is amiss – there's no mini-bar or bathrobe, for example, so arrive prepared.

Style 6, Atmosphere 6, Location 8

Quay Grand Suites *(right)*
61 Macquarie Street,
East Circular Quay
Tel: 02 9256 4000
www.mirvachotels.com
Rates: from AU$400

Comfortably treading the line between luxury hotel and serviced apartment, the Quay Grand Suites occupy a prime slice of Sydney real estate adjacent to the infamous so-called 'Toaster' building between Circular Quay wharf and the Opera House. There's a choice of one- or two-bedroom suites, each with separate bedrooms and all the tech necessities like flatscreen televisions, DVD/CD player and stereos. Though the décor lacks a certain pizzazz, the views from the opening windows and balconies are divine. The east-facing suites overlook the verdant Botanical Gardens, but it's the waterfront suites that overlook the Harbour Bridge that will bring a tear to your eye. If you're planning an extended stay, these suites are just the ticket. Each is equipped with washing machine, dryer and a modern kitchen – though you may not want to use it, given the tempting proximity to The Quadrant restaurant, which has floor-to-ceiling windows. Quay earns extra points for its recreation deck – along with a heated indoor swimming pool, there's a spa, sauna and gymnasium to work out that jet-lag.

Style 6, Atmosphere 7, Location 9

Ravesi's *(left)*
*118 Campbell Parade, corner
of Hall Street, Bondi Beach
Tel: 02 9365 4422
www.ravesis.com.au
Rates: AU$249–499*

Ravesi's is a little gem of a hotel smack-bang on the beachfront of Sydney's iconic Bondi Beach, well-loved by glamorous local A-listers who flock to the laid-back bar on the ground level, then head upstairs to the oh-so-chic Drift cocktail lounge, restaurant and wine bar on the second floor. However, the hotel's 12 rooms on the upper two levels also deserve applause. Designed by Dane van Bree in a breezy, elegant and contemporary style, each room has thick, chocolate-coloured carpet, crisp white linen, dark wood furniture and local artwork on the walls. Niceties include bathrobes, free wireless, flatscreen televisions and a well-stocked mini-bar (we love the tiny Belvedere Vodka bottle, Martini glasses and miniature cocktail shaker). For a glimpse of Sydney's body beautiful, the location across the road from the sands of Bondi Beach simply can't be beaten. Try to reserve one of the two beachfront rooms, which have double balcony doors that can be flung open to a view of the Pacific Ocean and Bondi's bronzed, bikini-clad locals sauntering around below. Our only one quibble is the slightly dated bathrooms

(after all, we do love to be sylish in the shower too).

Style 8, Atmosphere 8, Location 10

Sebel Pier One *(right)*
11 Hickson Road, The Rocks
Tel: 02 8298 9999
www.sebelpierone.com.au
Rates: from AU$220

With its waterfront location and uninterrupted harbour views, scarcely a weekend goes by when the Sebel isn't hosting a wedding. Set on a historic former wharf, the hotel was being refurbished at the time of writing which is welcome news as the interiors were looking a little dated (note our 6 Style rating), but rooms are luxuriously equipped in nautical tones of blue and hardwood furniture, with heritage wooden beams jutting across the ceilings. It's worth noting that some of the windows in the Heritage rooms are rather small. A much better option are the Waterside King rooms or the 62-square-metre Walsh Bay Suite, which has a fabulous day bed to lounge on that overlooks the harbour and even a telescope for a closer look at the yachts bobbing past. Not that you will spend much time indoors. There's the al fresco Front restaurant and bar on the wharf for a harbour-view sundowner, and the hotel is excellently placed for visitors wanting to explore the historic The Rocks precinct, with its

outdoor markets, patisseries and heritage pubs. Icons like Harbour Bridge are around 100 steps or so from the door. It's also a solid choice for anyone with a penchant for the arts, with the Sydney Theatre and Bangarra Dance Theatre a mere stroll away.

Style 6, Atmosphere 7, Location 9

Shangri-La *(top)*
176 Cumberland Street, The Rocks
Tel: 02 9250 6000
www.shangri-la.com/sydney
Rates: AU$230–5,000

Even purists will find it difficult to fault the Shangri-La. It's one of those hotels that has it all covered. Every square-centimetre is kitted out sumptuously with solid bathtubs, tasteful furnishings and modern art adorning the walls, while each suite boasts a water view over Sydney Harbour and beds so palatially comfortable you might be tempted to peak at the mattress label. On level 36 there's fine-dining at the one-hatted Altitude restaurant courtesy of chef Steven Krasicki, and vertiginous cocktails at the swanky Blu Bar, which has floor-to-ceiling windows overlooking the harbour. Downstairs all your pampering needs are met at CHI The Spa, a world-class Asian spa adjacent to the hotel's gym and indoor pool (see Play). With all of this on offer, it would seem a pity to set foot outside of the premises, but the hotel also happens to be in The Rocks and a short stroll through Sydney's historic streets will lead you to many of the city's top-end bars, restaurants and shops. The icing

on the cake is free wireless internet – a welcome change from the exorbitant fees charged at other five-star establishments. A fabulous, faultless hotel.

Style 9 Atmosphere 8 Location 9

Sheraton on the Park *(bottom)*
161 Elizabeth Street, CBD
Tel: 02 9286 6000
www.starwood.com
Rates: from AU$315

Directly fronting the verdant expanse of Hyde Park, the Sheraton is a good choice for travellers with extra luggage room, as it's within ambling distance from Sydney's department stores and the new Westfield shopping mall. Of the 557 guest rooms, including 48 suites, the better rooms face Hyde Park and enjoy a leafy aspect, but all are chic and contemporary, with black and cream tones, striking striped headboards, framed artwork, black marble bathrooms with separate bathtubs and Bvlgari products. The beds are all fitted with Sheraton Sweet Sleeper™ mattresses for marshmallow softness. Executive suites are nearly twice the size of standard rooms, but for those with a little more moolah to burn, check into one of the Terrace Suites on floors 16-21, which have private outdoor terraces with magnificent views over the treetops to St. Mary's Cathedral, walk-in wardrobes and far more entertaining space and amenities like dining tables, numerous lounges and BOSE sound systems. Expert massages and indulgent beauty treatments are available at the On The Park Rejuvenation spa on level 22, which has sweeping views over the city, as does the indoor rooftop swimming pool. The hotel gym is impressive – and you can burn off excess hedonism with personal trainers on-hand. For something less strenuous, The Conservatory Bar on level two is a classy watering hole, with high-back lounge chairs and two-storey windows overlooking the treetops.

Style 8, Atmosphere 7, Location 9

Sofitel *(left)*
61-101 Phillip Street, CBD
Tel: 02 9228 9188

www.sofitelsydney.com.au
Rates: from AU$250

The beds at Sofitel are famous, and quite rightly so. The patented mattresses are as spongy as fairy cakes, featuring a box spring design and a balance support mechanism created by dense, body-cocooning foam. It's just as well the hotel offers packages that encourage in-room dalliances, like the I Love Chocolate, which includes an all-chocolate hamper, and a late check-out. Or how about a private butler to serve you dinner, draw an aromatherapy bath and even arrange a private shopping experi-

ence? Perhaps an in-room visit from the nearby Chanel boutique? Part of the global Accor network, Sofitel has 436 rooms and although the décor is at the less snazzy end of the five-star scale, most overlook the circular central Garden Courtyard and all feature the sublime aforementioned beds, mod-cons and marble bathrooms equipped with Roger & Gallet products. It's worth upgrading to one of the luxury club rooms, which are larger and offer club access and additional niceties like Nespresso coffee machines and complimentary Evian water. Female travellers will especially enjoy the free passes to the Elixir health club on level one, which offers pilates reformer and yoga classes. There's also a Lattouf Hair Spa within the hotel, a blessing for those bad hair days.

Style 7, Atmosphere 7, Location 8

Star City   *(right)*
80 Pyrmont Street, Pyrmont
Tel: 02 9777 9000
www.starcity.com.au
Rates: AU$580–AU$990

At the time of writing this guide, Star City was in the midst of a multimillion-

dollar renovation. Stag parties and blokes intent on living our their rat-pack fantasies are waiting with baited breath for the 171-room, 5-star hotel, due in 2012. In the interim, wannabe high-rollers will have to make do with the current five-star accommodation, situated adjacent to the casino with its galaxy of slot machines, blackjack and roulette tables. Gambling may be the main drawcard to staying at Star City, but you don't need to know your Ace of Spades from your Queen of Hearts to benefit from this sprawling property, which houses some of Sydney's top restaurants and the stunning Astral Bar on Level 17, which serves breakfast by day and killer cocktails and a daz-zling view of Darling Harbour by night. Guests can even catch the latest mu-sical at the nearby Lyric Theatre (see Culture). Plus, Chinatown and the city's department stores are only a short stroll away. Along with hotel rooms, a smart option for travellers staying lon-ger are the Star Suites, equipped with a full-sized fridge, stove, microwave and laundry facilities, and not one, but three gargantuan plasma televisions - in the lounge, bedroom and above the spa in the bathroom.

Style 8, Atmosphere 7, Location 8

Tivoli Villa   *(opposite)*
Rose Bay
Tel: 02 9331 2881
www.housesandapartments.com.au
Rates: from AU$1,200

Tivoli Villa is described as The Great Gatsby mansion, and it's easy to see why. Set in the centre of the dress circle of the ritzy eastern suburbs, this sprawling property is reminiscent of F. Scott Fitzgerald's fictional mansion on Long Island's North Shore – with a little bit of Hollywood glitz and glamour to boot. Built in 1915, this prestigious har-bourfront mansion can be rented out exclusively, with five bedrooms and living and dining areas sprawled over three levels. The interiors highlight the property's original features like chande-liers, opulent Art Deco bathrooms and decorative cornices, brilliantly offset by a modern white palette, contemporary design furniture and magnificent, un-interrupted harbour views from each bedroom. You will want for nothing, with numerous televisions with cable and wireless internet throughout, an antique grand piano, space for four cars and even butler's quarters. Best of all, there's a huge outdoor swimming pool and poolside cabana – overlook-ing the stupendous vista of the harbour, of course. Jay Gatsby and his socialites would surely approve.

Style 10, Atmosphere 9, Location 7

eat…

You lucky, lucky devils – you're in for a treat. Sydney has one of the most exciting food industries in the world, a million miles from the 'shrimp on the barbie', Vegemite, Outback Steakhouse and Foster's beer ignominy it's suffered with for so long.

Australia's talented contemporary chefs are taking on the world with a cuisine we've dubbed 'Mod Oz' – where chefs cherry-pick the best of French, Italian or Japanese culinary genius and Australianise it. Check out the restaurants run by Sydney-based superchefs Neil Perry, Guillaume Brahimi, Justin North, Matt Moran, Mark Best and Tetsuya Wakuda. The city's chefs and gourmands owe a lot to the massive influx of Chinese, Thai, Vietnamese, Japanese and Malaysia immigrants because it's now reaping the benefits of a thriving Asian gastronomy scene. Those who can't get enough of sashimi should make a beeline for Sake or Sushi-e, while Chinatown should be on every culinary itinerary for *xiao long bao* dumplings at Din Tai Fung, Peking duck at Golden Century and barbecued pork from any one of the myriad eateries lining the streets. Food critics have waxed lyrical about the Thai cuisine, in particular, which Sydneysiders probably eat on average at least once a week – one even went as far as saying Sydney Thai food is the best in the world. It's true that Thai joints are a dime a dozen, but we've listed, in our opinion, the best the city has to offer with Sailors Thai, Longrain and Spice I Am, proof that you need not empty your wallet for beef massamam perfection.

But Sydney cannot deny its roots. There's a reason the world has heard of the famous Aussie barbecue, and that's because Australian beef is world-famous. There are 27-million beef cattle in the country and Australians manage to eat about 46.5kg of red meat each year in their backyards, at beach barbecues or in steakhouses – statistics that should light up the eyes of a visiting carnivore. Keep an eye out for Gunnadoo, Cape Grim, Sher or David Blackmore Wagyu, Greenhams and Rangers Valley, and don't forget to try the super-lean (less than two per cent fat) and delicious cuts of kangaroo.

Along with the red meat, pescetarians will fit right into Sydney's love affair for all things seafood. Whether you want to eat Yamba Bay prawns the size of your hand, tender white barramundi fillets, lobster or calamari – or crack open a bottle of Champagne with a platter of Sydney rock oysters – you've come to the right place. Sydneysiders are seafood snobs – you only need to spend an hour at the Seafood Market to see how spoiled we are – but Manta, Rockpool and Flying Fish never fail to impress.

Finally, you've heard about Australian wine. Here's your chance to test those exquisite drops from the Hunter Valley and Margaret River. Many of the eateries allow you to BYO – 'bring your own' – wine, but the finer ones have lists and sommeliers who know their craft inside out, so let them impress you.

our favourite restaurants...

Our favourites:
Duke Bistro 12
est.
Flying Fish
Guillaume at Bennelong
Marque
Otto Ristorante
Porteño
Rockpool Bar & Grill
Sushi e
Tetsuya's

For Food:
est.
Guillaume at Bennelong
Marque
Porteño
Rockpool Bar & Grill

For Service:
Flying Fish
Guillaume at Bennelong
Otto Ristorante
Rockpool Bar & Grill
Tetsuya's

For Atmosphere:
Bodega
Bloodwood
Duke Bistro
Porteno
Sushi e

For Australian Cuisine:
Aria
Bloodwood
Duke Bistro
est.
Marque

What's on the menu?

■ Ad Lib *(top)*
1047 Pacific Highway, Pymble
Tel: 02 9988 0120
www.adlibbistro.com
*Open: noon–3pm Mon–Fri, 5–10pm
Mon–Sat*
AU$80 *French*

The suburb of Pymble, with its leafy mansion-filled streets and expensive private schools, seemed an unlikely locale for an elegant French bistro because it's around a 20-minute drive from the CBD. But plonking a neighbourhood bistro in a neighbourhood makes sense, *non?* And it appears Sydneysiders are willing to travel for chef Dietmar Sawyere's food. With timber floors, the spacious, elegant dining room has a breezy atmosphere, with high-backed banquettes and tables scattered around to encourage con-

vivial conversations. Unfold the brown paper menu and say bonjour to a plate of Oscetria caviar, served with boiled quail eggs and a chilled shot of Belvedere vodka, and then bid your waistline *au revoir* with some French bistro soul food. The pig's trotter or onion soup gratinée is a crowd-pleaser, the duck pâté and onion marmalade combo is smoother than a Barry Manilow album, while main courses like duck confit, organic chicken escalope or an ocean trout fillet with garden peas and mint won't disappoint, either. Book ahead – it's nearly always full, something that hasn't changed despite the fact Sawyere opened his second Ad Lib in Double Bay (21 Bay Street, tel: 02 9988 0120) in late 2010.

Food 8, Service 8, Atmosphere 7

Aki's   *(left)*

1/6 Cowper Wharf Road,
Woolloomooloo
Tel: 02 9332 4600
www.akisindian.com.au
Open: noon–3pm, 6–10pm.
Closed Saturday lunch.

AU$100   *Indian*

You only need to look around at the other diners to order with confidence at Aki's. As possibly the sole fine-dining Indian establishment in Sydney, Aki's has the monopoly and is the second home of small groups of well-heeled Indian businessmen and British expatriates. The restaurant sits proudly at the helm of the Woolloomooloo wharf, often referred to as the Golden Mile, a prosperous waterfront nook packed with yachts, elite restaurants and even Hollywood stars like Russell Crowe, who lives upstairs in the penthouse apartments. With attentive native wait-staff and a refined atmosphere, chef Kumar Mahadevan has elevated Indian cuisine with flair, serving up rich, spicy dishes from his native Chennai to Goan seafood dishes like black tiger prawn curry. The tandoor oven gets a good work out – dishes like Achari Tikka, roasted chicken thigh fillets marinated in a sweet coat of yoghurt, ginger, fenugreek and lime are ordered steadily. Slightly messy but no less satisfying are the nacho-like Palak Patta chaat spinach leaves fried in crispy lentil batter – use them to scoop up a sweet mixture of chickpeas and potatoes doused in yoghurt, date, tamarind, chilli and mint. Wash it all down with a Kingfisher beer or cardapiriñha, a cardamon-infused

vodka cocktail with muddled limes, vanilla sugar and fresh mint.

Food 7, Service 8, Atmosphere 7

 Aria *(right)*
1 Macquarie Street,
East Circular Quay
Tel: 02 9252 2555
www.ariarestaurant.com
Open: noon–2.30pm, 5.30-10.30pm.
Closed Sat/Sun lunch.
AU$400 *Modern Australian*

One for the minted magnates, power-brokers and giddy couples toasting their new engagement, Aria is old-school fine-dining at its best. Set smack-bang on harbourfront at Circular Quay, it's a swanky affair with lots of heavy white linen, round tables and the ever-present views of the Harbour Bridge and Opera House. Owners Matt Moran and Peter Sullivan have worked out a winning formula with this elegant dining room and have nutted out some menu classics that have withstood the test of time. The Peking duck consommé – with its duck dumplings and shaved abalone – is a longstanding crowd-pleaser, as is the signature confit pork belly entrée, while whimsical desserts like coffee parfait and espresso ice-cream or Valrhona chocolate delice require your full attention (and the subtle unbuttoning of too-tight trousers). This is serious food and an excellent choice for splashing out. If there are more than four of you, try the Kitchen Table experience – an exclusive experience where diners sit in a private viewing area, watching the action hap-

eat...

Oysters St. Helen =3,50

Roast Pumpkin soup, Anise =12

Bouillabaisse =25
Mussel frites, bacon, shallot,
cream & parsley =25

NOT INCLUDED IN FORMULA
confit pork neck, pea, lardo,
Radish in emulsion

pening in the kitchen and sampling an eight-course tasting menu paired with wines.

Food 9, Service 9, Atmosphere 7

A Tavola *(top)*
348 Victoria Street, Darlinghurst
Tel: 02 9331 7871 www.atavola.com.au
Open: noon–3pm Friday only, 6pm–late Monday–Saturday
AU$80 *Italian*

This strip of Victoria Street is lined with a multitude of rather humdrum restaurants and a steady hum of pedestrian traffic. A Tavola stands out as one of the better choices – particularly for some of the best handmade pasta in Sydney. With a massive marble communal table crowning the room, mirrors and a blackboard of the daily menu chalked up on the wall, there's a buzzy, warm, elbow-to-elbow atmosphere in the main room and back section. After whetting your appetite on the baked olives – letting the warm oil drizzle over chunks of bread – and selecting some salads, like the Buffalo mozzarella, with rocket, vine-ripened tomatoes and prosciutto, pasta is on the agenda. A Tavola makes simple, homestyle Italian dishes – usually only three to choose from, like a twisted mess of spaghetti alle vongole, or *sigarette* with rabbit ragu. For desserts, there are classic dolce dishes of tiramisu and *affogato* to top it off.

Food 8, Service 8, Atmosphere 8

Baroque Bistro *(bottom)*
88 George Street, The Rocks
Tel: 02 9241 4811
www.baroquebistro.com.au
Open: daily, noon–late (4.30pm Sun)
AU$70 *Modern French*

Stylish and with an effervescent chi-chi, Baroque is all about well-priced French bistro fare in the heart of Sydney's historical quarter, The Rocks. Run by the charming Charkos family, who own nearby La Renaissance patisserie, Baroque serves quality bistro food in a bustling, stripped-back warehouse conversion space with Harbour Bridge views. Through eye-catching copper pots and pans that hang from the ceiling, diners get an eyeful of the action from the sprawling open kitchen; presided by Chef Peter Robertson, it pumps out starters like charcuterie boards with housemade rillettes, saucisson and terrine, washed down with a generous pour of pinot noir (oui oui) and served with fresh bread and extra virgin olive oil. Mains include French classics like bouillabaisse and meltingly soft duck confit, though given the family's 35-year patisserie expertise, it would be silly not to save room for dessert. Baroque's brightly-coloured macarons, in particular, have developed cult status in Sydney. In flavours like chocolate and passionfruit, pistachio and black cherry or the moreish salted caramel, they never fail to cause hysteria. Budding patissiers can even sign up to a Baroque macaron masterclasses if you want to learn how to make them yourself.

Food 8, Service 9, Atmosphere 8

Bathers Pavilion *(left)*
4 The Esplanade, Balmoral
Tel: 02 9969 5050
www.batherspavilion.com.au
Open: daily, noon–2pm, 6.30–8.30pm
AU$190 *Modern Australian*

This elegant restaurant is plonked rather primely on the million-dollar Balmoral Beach promenade, a mere metre (or is it two?) from the glistening harbour and frolicking beachgoers. One half of the iconic pavilion serves as a casual eatery, hugely popular for eggs benedict breakfasts and leisurely lunches, while the dining room on the other side is a smartly-dressed, white-clothed affair, setting the scene for Serge Dansereau's fresh, locally-sourced menu. From finely-sliced kingfish and pan-

seared scallops with boudin noir sprout pureé and walnut vinaigrette, to seared swordfish with South Australian calamari, the menu features a fabulous array of seafood, with meat dishes like roast guinea fowl and roast Gippsland lamb sating the carnivores. Fellow diners may not be the most vibrant (read: youthful) in town but it's a beautiful spot – and strolling along stunning Balmoral Beach to work off the white chocolate and pistachio chantilly feuilletine crunch, smothered with a dollop of bavarois crème and fresh raspberries, is an unbeatable way to top off an already fine meal.

Food 8, Service 8, Atmosphere 8

Becasse *(right)*
204 Clarence Street, CBD
Tel: 02 9283 3440
www.becasse.com.au
Open: noon–2.30pm, 6–10.30pm.
Closed Sat lunch and Sundays.
AU$250   *European*

With luxurious, heavy curtains and a rather serious-looking dining room tiered over one level and a mezzanine, Becasse may look like the sort of place old money comes to eat and sign billion-dollar contracts over business lunches, but forget appearances because the food is worth forgoing them. Chef and owner Justin North's artful, thoughtful menu has been wowing gastronomes since time immemorial, his outstanding French cuisine and dedication to seasonal produce never failing to floor critics, such as the milk-fed veal baked in coffee and clay or caramelised suckling pig and braised pork tail with roast parsnip and compressed apple. Keep an eye on the website as North occasionally holds special degustation nights with a focus on regional areas of France, such as Burgundy or Bordeaux, along with the popular monthly Cellar Night, where patrons can bring their own bottle of wine to dinner and have their corkage waived. Should you wish to select something from the menu, rest assured you're in safe hands with Georgia North, Justin's wife, who not only manages the front of house, but is also the sommelier.

Food 9 Service 8 Atmosphere 7

 Bentley Restaurant & Bar *(left)*
320 Crown Street, Surry Hills
Tel: 02 9332 2344
www.thebentley.com.au
Open: noon–5pm, 5–10.30pm Tues–Sat
AU$170 *Modern Australian*

In early 2010, the Bentley Bar had a Cinderella moment; Pascale Gomes-McNabb transformed the corner, Crown Street pub into a very stylish, slick eatery in the beating heart of Surry Hills, with glossy timber floors, hardwood furniture and paper design lamps hung artfully from the ceiling. The bar area is divided from the dining room where grown-up media types and fashion buyers like to sup vino and snack on tapas, which are a little pricey for most of the area's stovepipe jean-wearing hipsters. For diners, Chef Brent Savage's menu is raved about in culinary circles – the eight-course dining menu offers contemporary cuisine with imaginative flair, such as parmesan custard with truffled asparagus, black sesame and pea fondant with snow peas and goat's curd or Jerusalem artichoke tart with nettle sauce, pine mushrooms and

artichokes. It's all top-notch nosh, and with one of Sydney's most thought out wine lists, this is chic Surry Hills dining at its best.

Food 8, Service 9, Atmosphere 8

 Berta *(middle)*
17-19 Alberta Street, Surry Hills
Tel: 02 9264 6133
www.berta.com.au
Open: noon–3pm Fri only, 6–10.30pm Mon–Sat
AU$70 *Italian*

You'll need Google Maps to find this little gem but it's worth the hunt. Duck up a side street and squeeze into one of Surry Hills' growing stable of funky haunts, packed elbow-to-elbow and quite literally humming with diners. But make it early – because this tucked-away treasure doesn't take bookings and hanging around a laneway when you're hungry is a one-way ticket to a bad mood. Inside, Berta has dillusions of grandeur with cleverly-placed mirrors making it seem larger than reality,

but it's chaotic nevertheless and best avoided if you're searching for an intimate tête-à-tête. The blackboard specials chalked up on the wall and wine list are both an homage to all things Italian, with small plates of suckling pig, lentils or lamb, and the deliciously warming oxtail broth with wild green tortellini. Everything is designed to share and is reasonably priced. Even the wine is affordable – which might explain the maddening queues – but don't leave without testing out the heavenly cocktail of Prosecco with campari sorbet. La dolce vita in a glass.

Food 9, Service 8, Atmosphere 9

Bilson's   *(right)*
Radisson Plaza Hotel Sydney,
27 O'Connell Street, CBD
Tel: 02 8214 0496
www.bilsonsrestaurant.com
Open: noon–3pm Friday only, 6–10pm Tues–Sat
AU$240   *French*

The bar is set high when dining at Bilson's, due to the culinary powerhouse of owner Tony Bilson, known as the 'Godfather of Australian Cuisine', and chef Alfonso Alese who earned his stripes at El Bulli, Eugénie-les-Bains and Château Cordeillan Barges. Dining here is an intrinsically European experience that pushes boundaries, with excellent wine and smart interiors to match. White-clothed tables sit astride large Georgian windows with eye-catching canary yellow light fittings and artwork adorning the walls. As for the cuisine, the restaurant is based around changing tasting menus that draw inspiration from fresh Australian produce ranging from locally-sourced seafood and meat to the freshest vegetables zipped from farm to table. The size of the menus range from a paltry six, up to a truly gluttonous 15 in the wonderfully named 'Epiphanie – Presque Quatre'. Each course from each menu is painstakingly paired with suitable wines and the waiterstaff carefully explain the nuances of each of the dishes. For those who need to enjoy their food in a little more privacy, and why would you when

75

a little more privacy, and why would you when your coiffured clientele are as genteel as they are, then there is a small private dining room for special occasions. Once you've managed to roll our of the door, and roll you will, why not try a cocktail at Hemmesphere (see Drink) in the Establishment hotel nearby.

Food 9, Service 8, Atmosphere 8

Bistro Moncur *(left)*
116 Queen Street, Woollahra
Tel: 02 9327 9713
www.woollahrahotel.com.au
Open: noon–3pm, 6–10.30pm (9pm Sun). Closed Monday lunch.
AU$80 *French*

One of the Eastern Suburb's most iconic restaurants, Bistro Moncur has not lost any of its popularity since opening in 1993 – the place is perennially packed due to chef Damien Pignolet's classic Parisian bistro cuisine and smart, elegant dining room. Set on a bustling street in a leafy, well-to-do area of Woollahra (Sydney's version of Primrose Hill), the restaurant is pleasingly airy, with polished timber, crafty use of mirrored walls and eye-catching black-and-white mural artwork by Michael Fitzgames. The dining crowd is more old money than noveau riche, with a fair few purple-hued coiffed hairstyles about, but there's not a hint of snobbery – Bistro Moncur is simply about classic French food paired with a beautiful wine list, with the added bonus of an attached pub, the Wollahra

eat...

Hotel. Menu highlights abound, but particular stand-outs are the Provencale fish soup served with *rouille* and dainty croutons or the incredibly rich, fluffy onion soufflé, smothered with Gruyere cheese and paired with a 2008 Chateau Fuisse White Burgundy.

Food 8, Service 9, Atmosphere 8

Bloodwood *(right)*
416 King Street, Newtown
Tel: 02 9557 7699
www.bloodwoodnewtown.com.au
Open: 5pm–10.30pm Mon, Weds, Thurs;
noon–11pm (10pm Sun) Fri–Sun
AU$100 ***Modern Australian***

Could the grungy, eclectic suburb of Newtown be on its culinary way? For too long, the long and bustling King Street strip – famous for its pubs, thrift stores and quirky boutiques – has been weighed down with endless nondescript Thai eateries, but Bloodwood has upped the ante. With brilliant yellow piping, recycled timber floors, exposed brick, chaotic lightbulbs hanging from the ceiling and the clatter and buzz of an open kitchen, Bloodwood's industrial chic outfit is far from boring – and neither is the food, thanks to the trio of talents from chefs and owners Jo Ward, Mitchell Grady and Claire van Vuuren, who each have notably nodworthy resumes. Start with delightfully crunchy-yet-tender polenta chips with gorgonzola dipping sauce, move onto crisply-fried bean curd roll stuffed with juicy morsels of crab, pork and shiitake mushrooms, and go from there

77

to lamb *crepinette* or baked kingfish. It's little wonder the place is heaving nearly every night – book ahead.

Food 8, Service 9, Atmosphere 9

 Boca *(top)*
308-310 Liverpool Street, Darlinghurst
Tel: 02 9332 3373
www.boca.com.au
Open: 12.30–3pm Sat–Sun, 6–10pm (11pm Fri–Sat) Tues–Sun
AU$90 **Argentinean**

With brightly-painted scarlet walls and gold-framed portraits of fatty football legend Diego Maradona and Eva Perón adorning the walls, the dining room of Marcelo Berezowski and Santiago Correa's Argentinean grillhouse is warm, buzzy and inviting – unless, of course, you happen to be a vegetarian. If you're not, the mouthwatering smell of meats cooking over the authentic *parilla* (charcoal grill) is sensational. As a traditional Argentinean grill house, it's all about the meat here, salted up and cooked to perfection in the way Argentineans are famous for – from ribs, to sirloin inside skirt and chicken, all served on a slab of wood with an assortment of chunky dips like *chimichirri*. Sit at the downstairs bar to watch the grillmaster on a stool seat or grab a table upstairs in the dining room. Choose from one of the ten different *parrilladas* and order the house wine with your meal, which appears, oddly enough, in a penguin-shaped jug.

Food 7, Service 7, Atmosphere 8

 Bodega *(bottom)*
Shop 1/216 Commonwealth Street, Surry Hills
Tel: 02 9212 7766
www.bodega.com.au
Open: noon–2pm Thurs–Fri, 6–10pm Mon–Sat
AU$100 **Tapas**

There's barely room to swing a cat in this tiny, loud tapas joint, owned by chef/owners Ben Millgate and Elvis Abrahanowicz, who also own hugely popular Argentinean restaurant Porteno. With a colourful mural on the wall that proclaims 'Full belly, content heart', and a gregarious vibe, the place can fill up quickly with Surry Hills locals, who converge in throngs in a clatter of small plates and clinking glasses. There's plenty of bread and oil to go around, and the way to do Bodega is to order wide and a varied selection of small plates. Try the perennial favourites – the Argentinean-style *empanadas*, *piquillo* peppers stuffed with Bacala, a salad of octopus, and a Spanish chorizo and kipfler potatoes. All plates range from AU$6 up to AU$32 – around three should fill you up. Wash it down with excellent cocktails like the Surly Temple, a tangy refresher made with fresh passionfruit, mint and lime shaken with Zytnia Vodka, Liquor 43 and orange. All in all, fun and tasty stuff.

Food 9, Service 8, Atmosphere 9

La Boheme (left)
332 Darling Street, Balmain
Tel: 02 9810 0829
www.laboheme.net.au
Open: 6–11pm Mon–Thurs; 11am–midnight Fri; 8am–midnight Sat; 8am–10pm Sun

AU$70 **Czech**

European soul food, La Boheme's rich, salty and meat-driven dishes are lips-mackingly bohemian and the vaulted ceilings and delightfully warm interiors of the refurbished Lecture Hall at the Working Men's Institute have all the atmosphere of a Prague pub. The Czech Republic's cuisine gets a bad rap from its haughty Euro neighbours, but sitting in the Eastern European surrounds and washing down all the goodness with a chilled, cracking Pilsner, we beg to differ. Start with a slices of duck livers with sautéed onion and rye bread, and carve your own meltingly soft pork knuckle with crackling golden skin – smear it with horseradish and mustard, that's how they do it in Prague. Then move onto expertly-roasted duck with spongey soft dumplings and gravy, and the ubiquitous *schnitzel* and *sauerkraut*. Whatever you choose, it's flavourful stuff so arrive at this friendly Balmain restaurant with an appetite.

Food 8, Service 8, Atmosphere 8

Bootleg (right)
175 Victoria Street, Potts Point
Tel: 02 9361 3884
Open: 5–11pm (1am Thurs–Sat, 10pm Sun). Closed Mondays.

AU$70 **Italian**

With black-and-white photographs of New York, rockers and celebrities, such as Debbie Harry, adorning the walls, captured by NY-based photographer Janette Beckman, Bootleg has a touch of Manhattan cool about it. There's barely any elbow room in the narrow street-level bar and Italian eatery, but it's become quite the trendy neighbourhood hang-out for Potts Point locals on their way home from work and in the mood for a casual bite, a glass of wine and a catch up with friends. It's far enough from the seedier side of Kings Cross to be able to sit unharrassed on the tables and chairs assembled on the leafy footpath, while indoors there are bar stools and a limited number of leather booths facing the bar. Squeeze into one and order from the tapas-style menu, which serves up everything from cheeses, cured meats and crostini to more substantial dishes like lasagna.

Food 8, Service 8, Atmosphere 9

Buzo Trattoria (bottom)
3 Jersey Road, Woollahra
Tel: 02 9328 1600
www.buzorestaurant.com.au
Open: 6–11pm Mon–Sat

AU$150 **Italian**

This cosy, chic Italian restaurant is crammed with people on a nightly basis, and you might have to shuffle along to make room for your neighbouring diner on one of the low banquettes – if you get a table, that is. Set inside a corner terrace in leafy Woollahra, with bottles of wine, colourful Italian aperitifs displayed in hardwood racks and a cheerful staff chatting to customers,

Buzo is a neighbouhood place – the sort that is nearly always abuzz. It's a perfect for spending an evening nattering with a friend, elbows on tables, downing one, two or three glasses of wine and sharing some snacky *aperitivo* plates. Tear apart the supple buffalo mozzarella with some crostini and salami, followed by a few small plates of pan-fried lamb's kidneys, porcini mushroom and truffle lasagne. Everything is designed to share, but you may not feel so generous at dessert. The tangy pomegranate, raspberry and Prosecco granita or baked lemon cheesecake is strictly for one (at least, that's what you say to your dining partner).

Food 8, Service 8, Atmosphere 9

China Doll   *(top)*
4/6 Cowper Wharf Road,
Woolloomooloo
Tel: 02 9380 6744
www.chinadoll.com.au
Open: daily, noon–3pm, 6–10.30pm
AU$180   ***Modern Asian***

During the day, cashed-up power brokers love to lunch at China Doll, exchanging talk of falling stocks, hedge funds or property coups between sips of crisp New Zealand sauvignon blanc and mouthfuls of exceptional Sichuan-style salt and pepper prawns. Located on the Woolloomooloo finger wharf alongside a host of fine restaurants, it's an idyllic spot during the day with water views, the gleaming sight of million-dollar yachts and well-coiffed, lunching ladies tottering past. The Iain Halliday-designed restaurant is slick and glamorous, with a striking mural

and an expertly-trained staff, with smartly turned-out waiters gliding about polishing glasses and bending over backwards to cater to your every whim. Though the name suggests Chinese and Chinese only, chef Frank Shek is influenced by all Asian flavours and dabbles with all styles from Penang and Bangkok to Hong Kong, featuring drunken chilli beef, chilli salt and pepper squid, crunchy green papaya salad and delicate wonton dumplings. The wine list is exceptional and at night, China Doll is equally seductive, with the glittering city skyline backdrop and an inventive 'yin and yang' cocktail list.

Food 8 Service 8 Atmosphere 8

The Commons   *(bottom)*
32 Burton Street, Darlinghurst
Tel: 02 9358 1487
www.thecommons.com.au
Open: 6pm–late Tues/Weds; noon–
late Thurs/Fri; 8am–late Sat/Sun
AU$50   ***European***

The Commons is a favourite for the local stovepipe jean- and chequered shirt-wearing crowd that congregates for casual boozing in the sandstone-walled courtyard, which has lots of overhanging greenery and flickering candles at night. Set in a heritage terrace, complete with recycled hardwood floors, the restaurant is laidback and wholesome, with an organic, rotating menu that's fairly heavy with meat dishes like rabbit terrine, beef ragu and just-like-mamma-used-to-make-a lasagna. It's cheap enough to attract a younger, friendly crowd, and though there's a limited number of communal

dining tables, good-natured diners are usually happy to shunt over to make room. It's convivial enough to order some antipasti at the bar and wait until there's some space – either pull up a stool or a wooden crate in the court-yard, or in winter, head down to the cosy sandstone cellar. There's a small bar tucked away downstairs that serves unusual wines and single-malt whiskies with deep leather chairs, a growing col-lection of books in the library and even a fireplace to encourage lingering.

Food 7, Service 7, Atmosphere 8

 **The Corner House** *(left)*
281 Bondi Road, Bondi
Tel: 02 8020 6698
www.thecornerhouse.com.au
Open: daily, 5pm–late
AU$80   ***Pizza / Italian***

The only place in Sydney where you can hack at a pizza with scissors – a curiously gratifying experience, trust us – this relaxed Bondi ristorante attracts a steady stream of hip local residents. Diners in the cosy front room nestle un-der a wall of wine bottles, and to reach the rear dining room, with its honey-coloured Chesterfield banquettes, you have to sneak through the kitchen – a quirk that owner Anthony Kaplan in-tended, to emulate a hip, devil-may-care New York 'tude. Upstairs there's

an intimate cocktail bar with a balcony for balmy nights. Though famous for the DIY chopping of wood-fired pizzas (go for the Crowded House – quattro staggioni style with quarters of salami, anchovies, sautéed mushrooms and buffalo, provolone and fontina cheeses), the kitchen also serves up more complex fare including pork belly or spatchcock. There's a decent wine list written on brown paper and pegged to the table – try something from the 'crowd-pleaser' section, like the Delta Vineyard pinot noir from New Zealand.

Food 7, Service 8, Atmosphere 9

<table>
<tr><td>Cut Bar & Grill</td><td>(right)</td></tr>
</table>

16 Argyle Street, The Rocks
Tel: 02 9259 5695
www.cutbarandgrill.com
Open: noon–3pm Mon–Fri,
daily, 6–10pm
AU$160   ***Steakhouse***

Steak has never been so hip. With its moody lighting, butcher's block chopping board tables and meat cleavers instead of handles on the bathroom doors, Sydney's newest steakhouse oozes cool. The décor is courtesy of young design duo Luchetti Krell, who transformed this heritage-listed, cellar-style space into a chic New York-inspired restaurant. It's become a hot ticket for the city's well-heeled carnivores and banker boys' nights

out, with lots of intimate nooks, cow-hide leather chairs, banquettes and room dividers creating intimacy – and excellent music and cocktails to boot. It's not all about red meat, either, with another focus on sustainable seafood cooked on a wood-fired grill, though it's a challenge to order anything but the famed Sher Wagyu. Sourced from a farm in Victoria, this soft, marbled beef is revered around the world and it's near impossible not to be seduced by the tantalising sight of a four-hour slowroasted, fleshy, fatty grade-7 hunk of it, rolled around on a beef trolley between tables by waitstaff. There are other cuts, too, including grain-fed beef, with a tasting plate for those who can't choose. All beef is cooked on a char-coal- and hardwood-fired grill and then broiled on a 650-degree celsius broiler. With a superb range of sides like broccoli with toasted almonds, organic peas with onion and mint or shoestring fries, it's a carnivore's unadulterated fantasy.

Food 7, Service 9, Atmosphere 9

Din Tai Fung *(left)*
Level 1, World Square Shopping Centre, 644 George Street, CBD
Tel: 02 9264 6010
Open: daily, 11.30am (11am Sat/sun)–2.30pm (3pm Sat/Sun), 5.30 (5pm Thurs–Sun)–9pm (9.30pm Thurs–Sat),
AU$50 *Chinese*

This is the only Din Tai Fung operating in Australia, and there's a massive banner reminding you of this auspicious fact hung proudly outside the door. Get here well before the hunger pangs set in because it doesn't take bookings and this hugely popular Tapei chain is rightly famous for its dumplings. On any given day, or night, there'll be queues stretching out the door, though you can watch the action through the glass display kitchen as a fascinating production line of around ten scrubs-and-mask wearing workers make dumplings. They need to pump these out as quickly as they can, because the pork, crabmeat and *xiao long bao* (Shanghai soup dumplings) are, in a word, lifechanging. Diners will patiently wait an hour and happily sit elbow-to-

elbow at communal tables for these hot, steamy bundles of joy. They taste even better when dunked into balsamic vinegar and doused in a spoonful of chilli sauce. Wash your meal down with one of the fruity cocktails or a chilled Tsingtao beer.

Food 9, Service 7, Atmosphere 7

Duke Bistro *(right)*
65 Flinders Street, Darlinghurst
Tel: 02 9332 3180
www.dukebistro.com.au
Open: 7pm–midnight (1am Thurs, 2am Fri/Sat) Tues–Sat
AU$80   ***Modern Australian***

With common tables, floral banquettes, bright green walls and a suitably fashion-forward Darlinghurst crowd, the Duke wears the current hipster crown and it's no surprise given the booming medley of talented staff, from Thomas Lim (ex-Tetsuya's), Mitch Orr (2010 Young Chef of the Year) and booze trio Charles Ainsbury, Andy Penney and Joel Amos creating potent cock-

tails. It's a hip hangout and the food is delicious – deep-fried chicken wings with coleslaw, sardines and baby globe artichokes, white anchovies on grilled baguette, a cucumber and ogo sea-weed salad sprinkled with sesame – and quirky dishes that throw food and booze together remarkably well – like the king-fish gin and tonic, a delightful blend of finely-sliced sashimi and cucumber, and a G&T jelly made from Hendrick's Gin. Best of all, it's just upstairs from the dive bar-style Flinders (see Drink), where the Eastern Suburbs' collective party until dawn, knocking back cocktails and the almighty pickleback. We like it – a lot.

Food 8, Service 9, Atmosphere 9

Efendy   *(left)*
79 Elliott Street, corner of
Darling Street, Balmain
Tel: 02 9810 5466
www.efendy.com.au
Open: noon (9am Sat / Sun)–10pm.
Closed Mondays.
AU$70   **Turkish**

Efendy will change your mind about Turkish cuisine, which isn't raved about enough to our mind. Set in a renovated Victorian homestead, with stained-glass windows and a pretty courtyard, this neighbourhood Balmain restaurant is ideally placed to share snacky plates with a group of friends and remember those heady nights in Istanbul. Mezze to share is the order of the day; order four apiece and a main and eat with gusto. It's all delicious stuff, like fat,

juicy prawns, a spicy lamb kofte on warm *hummus* or the splendidly-named 'efendy begendi', which is a four-hour 'Yahni' slow-braised beef cheek with olives and smoky eggplant purée. Drinkswise, try some Efes Pilsen Turkish beer or 'raki' – the dubious yet potent Turkish spirit. All meals should finish with thick, sludgy Turkish coffee while you nibble on fragrant squares of *lokum*, a traditional Turkish sweet, and if there's still room (there's always room) for a nightcap, you're in luck. Balmain has one of the highest concentrations of excellent pubs per capita and you're in stumbling distance from many of the good 'uns like The London or The Exchange.

Food 8, Service 7, Atmosphere 8

est. *(right)*

Level 1, 252 George Street, CBD
Tel: 02 9240 3000 www.merivale.com
Open: noon–2.30pm, 6–10pm.
Closed Sat lunch and Sundays.

AU$380   ***Modern Australian***

The sort of place where diners rubberneck to see who else is around, est. consistently wins gongs in every restaurant and food award over the years, and rightfully wears its crown as one of Sydney's finest restaurants, wining and dining status-seeking city elite with faultless cuisine by chef Peter Doyle and a wine list to impress the most discerning vinophile. It would be difficult to find a flaw in the slick, sophisticated service or anything on the menu, though the five-course degustation highlights the best on offer. Start with freshly-shucked oysters and then select from a seasonal menu, featuring anything from expertly-grilled Rangers Valley beef lightly served with wasabi-imbued butter, or a pan-roasted lamb rib-eye atop a medley of artichoke hearts, broad beans and delicate watercress. There are four selections to choose from with each course, but when you get to the cheese it would be foolish to choose anything except the fabulous La Luna matured organic goats' cheese, sourced from a tiny farm just outside of Melbourne and served with nashi pear and almonds. As for desserts, the passion fruit soufflé, which arrives with a tangy passion fruit sorbet, will have you gushing for weeks. All in all, est. is a discerning establishment for those who think credit crunch

is a type of breakfast cereal. Eyewatering prices, mouthwatering cuisine.

Food 10, Service 9, Atmosphere 7

 Etch *(left)*
62 Bridge Street, CBD
Tel: 02 9247 4777
www.etchdining.com
Open: noon (5pm Sat)–11pm.
Closed Sundays.
AU$160 **Modern European**

Tucked beneath the InterContinental hotel, this French dining room is a CBD hideaway with elegant hardwood dining chairs and swirly, patterned wallpaper, and a staff that knows the difference between hovering and being attentive. Owner Justin North and

Chef James Metcalfe pride themselves on locally-sourced, sustainable food and the menu features modern European fare with influences from southern and regional France and Italy and Spain's Basque and Catalan region. Featuring Gundooee grass-fed organic beef, Game Farm quail and De Costi seafood, it's as much of a pleasure knowing there's a relationship and respect for the way produce reaches the plate as it is eating it. Try the seven-course delight paired with a wine hand-selected by sommelier Katherine Sherman, but don't forget to order a cocktail before you dine – the Dirty Hot Martini of gin, black pepper and Sicilian olives is a saucy start to the night.

Food 8, Service 9, Atmosphere 8

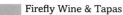

Firefly Wine & Tapas *(right)*
Promenade, Pier 7,
17 Hickson Road, Walsh Bay
Tel: 02 9241 2031
www.fireflybar.com.au
Open: 11am–11pm Mon–Sat
AU$60 ***Tapas***

A busy little wine bar with a fantastic vibe and smiley staff, Firefly's tables are usually abuzz with Sydney theatre-goers engrossed in pre- or post-show conversation. There's a lot to please, from the cracking view of expensive yachts moored at Walsh Bay to tasty wine and beguiling tapas, such as the duck pancakes with crunchy bean sprouts, shallots and water chestnuts, spiced chickpea fritters with aoli and tomato salsa, or succulent kingfish ceviche. If you can't decide, get the shared banquet and order a drop from the rotating wine and beer list. In Sydney, you can't be waterside sans cocktail, either, and Firefly makes sure there's plenty to choose from, like the Rumba Tiki, made from Appleton rum, pineapple juice, coconut syrup, sage and muddled pineapple. Those in the mood for theatre, a couple of glasses of red and a chin-wag will love this place – it's so popular, there are already two more venues in Lane Cove (24 Burns Bay Rd, tel: 02 9420 1629) and Neutral Bay (24 Young Street, tel: 02 9909 0193), both north of the Harbour Bridge.

Food 8, Service 9, Atmosphere 8

■ **Flying Fish** *(left)*
Lower Deck, Jones Bay Wharf,
19-21 Pirrama Road, Pyrmont
Tel: 02 9518 6677
www.flyingfish.com.au
Open: noon–2.30pm, 6–10.30pm. Closed
Mondays, except summer dinners.
AU$180 **Seafood**

Easily one of the slickest seafood joints in the city, diners get an eyeful of passenger cruisers, yachts and ferries gliding past at this stunning, two-storey harbourside loft restaurant. Aside from the distracting water views, the restaurant has a stylish outfit, with high, vaulted beams stretching above, heritage windows and a clever wall of wine display. Restaurant designer Michael McCann went to town when he commissioned Pam Morris to create two individual glass pendant sculpture chandeliers – the eye-catching 270-globe light sculpture suspended from the ceiling is aptly called 'Reef Spawn'. As for the seafood, rest assured the fish couldn't be more fresh had you leaned over and plucked it from the harbour yourself. Whether it's an array of finely-sliced sashimi,

a blue eye, flathead, poached scampi or Chef Peter Kuruvita's signature Sri Lankan prawn curry (he grew up there), everything is artfully presented and the sommeliers know their craft – it's a joy to eat here.

Food 9, Service 9, Atmosphere 8

■ **Four in Hand** *(middle)*
105 Sutherland Street, Paddington
Tel: 02 9362 1999
www.fourinhand.com.au
Open: noon–2.30pm, 6.30–10pm
(9pm Sun). Closed Mondays.
AU$80 **French**

As the old adage goes, don't judge a book by its cover. Four in Hand may technically be a pub, but the food is anything but pub grub. Irish chef Colin Fassnidge has created a loyal following among the gastronomes for excellent modern cuisine in this iconic Paddington pub, served the way it should be: big on natural flavour, classic and wholesome. Decadent groups can order the famous whole suckling pig (at AU$80 a head) but the à la carte menu

is perfect for a long, leisurely lunch. If you're in a pair, snuggle into a smart leather banquette in the cosy dining room and order the slow-braised lamb shoulder with kipfler roast potatoes, or the fall-apart-in-your-mouth, 12-hour braised beef shin, Bourguignon-style. Anything seafood or vegetarian is almost an afterthought here, but if you love meaty, French Bistro-style dishes you won't be disappointed.

Food 8, Service 8, Atmosphere 7

Golden Century *(right)*
393-399 Sussex Street, CBD
Tel: 02 9212 3901
www.goldencentury.com.au
Open: daily, noon–3.30am
AU$50 *Chinese*

As one of Sydney's favourite late-night dining venues, Golden Century has a cult-like following and the mere mention of it to a local will induce an enthusiastic, "Oh, I love that place!" From the gigantic tanks by the door that teem with lobster, mud crabs and sorrowful schools of fish, to the gaudy carpet,

gold furniture and sturdy white table-cloths, this is classic Chinese restaurant at its best, and the place is abuzz even at 2.30am with Chinese families, hungry nightclubbers and buck's nights. The uninitiated may wonder why this sprawling Chinese restaurant is so popular, given the frustrating queues and the exasperating service, but don't be put off by the infuriating nonchalance of the staff. Do as Sydneysiders do; wave them down, bark your order and tuck into a chilled Tsingtao while you wait. It'll be worth it, we promise. If you're in a group, order Peking duck – request half to wrap in pancakes and the rest served up as *san choi bow*. If you're solo, the scallops stir-fried with vegetables, fried rice or mud crab served Szechuan-style or with ginger and shallots are all as good at 2am as they are 7pm, especially with a big old plate of garlicky *gai laan* greens.

Food 8, Service 5, Atmosphere 8

Guillaume at Bennelong *(left)*

Sydney Opera House, Bennelong Point
Tel: 02 9241 1999
www.guillaumeatbennelong.com.au
Open: noon–3pm Thurs/Fri,
5.30–11pm Mon–Sat

AU$450   *French*

Nestled smugly on its lofty perch within the Opera House's southern sail and overlooking Circular Quay's buzzing harbour, the mere mention of this restaurant will elicit a lusty sigh from any Sydneysider. French chef Guillaume Brahimi's illustrious career has spanned continents, and though launching more award-winning restaurants than you can poke a forkful of foie gras at, his namesake creation is truly fine-dining at its very best. With soaring, vaulted ceilings and dramatic glass windows, the dining room is divided into intimate tables mostly frequented by glitzy Eastern Suburbs doyens and the famous and the fortunate. Waiters glide, pirouette and would probably execute triple somersaults to please, and the food is, in a word, exquisite. For mere mortals, the nine-course degustation paired with either Australian or French wine will leave you broke, yet floating happily in another stratosphere altogether. Blow out on gently seared scallops served with cauliflower purée and salivatingly marbled, grade-nine Wagyu rib-eye and finish with a zesty explosion in the form of a sweet, fruity soup with tangy mango sorbet and lime marshmallows. It couldn't possibly get any better – unless, of course, if Guillaume spoonfed it to you himself.

Food 10, Service 9, Atmosphere 8

eat...

Hugos Manly *(right)*
Shop 1, Manly Wharf,
East Esplanade, Manly
Tel: 02 8116 8555
www.hugos.com.au
Open: daily, noon (11.30am Sat/Sun)–
late
AU$100 *Italian/Pizza*

The so-hip-it-hurts Hugos Bar Pizza in King's Cross (see next entry) is a firm favourite for Sydney's glitterati, but Manly got a mozzarella-coated slice of the action, too, when celebrity chef Pete Evans decided to open a sprawling, waterside venue in Manly. Balanced on the end of the pier next to the Manly Ferry Wharf, the timber-decked terrace and open-air concertina doors offer a beguiling vista of the sparkling harbour and ferries chugging in the distance. Expect a lengthy wait for a table, which are low-slung, backed leather banquettes and tables, though there are high stools and benches near the bar if you want to down a cocktail or a glass of wine while you wait. There's a good deal of primping and preening among the clientele, but on a balmy day it's one of the buzziest spots on the promenade. Culinary offerings focus on Italian classics like pastas and seafood, and while everything is well-priced, of high quality and served with a subtle zhuzzing, the premium pizza is where it's at – go for the fig, pancetta, gorgonzola and basil.

Food 8, Service 8, Atmosphere 9

Hugos Bar Pizza *(left)*
33 Bayswater Road, Kings Cross
Tel: 02 9332 1227
www.hugos.com.au
Open: 5pm (3pm Sun)–late.
Closed Mondays.
AU$80 *Pizza*

Just downstairs from its sister venue – the frivolous, party palace that is Hugos Lounge – Hugos Bar Pizza sits elegantly on a split-levelled terrazzo with a view of the passers-by trickling down Bayswater Road. Perched unassumingly in the eye of the Kings Cross red-light and nightclub storm, if you're chomping into your mozzarella-laden Neapolitan-style Pork Belly pizza on a weekend, you're in for a people-watching treat. Call ahead to snag yourself space on the outdoor leather banquette, though the interior is just as slick. With a backlit marble bar and sunken loungey area, the concertina-style windows facing the street are thrown open on balmy nights. As for the food, Hugos is owned by celebrity chef Pete Evans, with premium pizza, a range of Italian-inspired entrées and mains like hearty Italian pasta dishes,

Waygu beef and seafood. But it would be silly to order anything aside from the pizza – the aforementioned Pork Belly with slow-roasted pork belly, sweet and sour onions and radicchio is a particular standout.

Food 8, Service 8, Atmosphere 9

Icebergs *(middle)*
1 Notts Avenue, Bondi Beach
Tel: 02 9365 9000
Open: noon–4.30pm, 6.30pm–midnight.
Closed Mondays.
AU$150 *Mediterranean*

If you want to take a brag-worthy snap of yourself to post on Facebook, this is the place. The glamorous Ms. Icebergs has teased and wooed Sydney's beautiful people for years with its megawatt ocean views and so-chic-it-hurts wait-staff clad in white tuxedos and outfits by Australian designer Kirrily Johnston. The floor-to-ceiling glass windows and balcony overlook Bondi Icebergs swimming pool and crashing waves – rest assured everyone from Cate Blanchett to Rupert Murdoch has sat here, swill-

eat...

ing fine wine or imported Italian beers and gazing appreciatively out to sea. The bar is a fine spot to share snacky plates and a drink as you swing in a hanging cane chair or banquette, but the modern light Mediterranean fare served in the restaurant is where culinary magic happens. In the seductive, dimly-lit dining room facing the ocean, service is exemplary; the waitstaff is able to rattle off an astonishing array of seasonal specials and details about each dish and materialise within a millisecond of when your glass needs a top-up. The black-as-the-night squid ink risotto is a highlight, as is the tender 150-day grain-fed Angus/Hereford rib-eye steak and classic zesty sgroppino – made for sharing. Whatever you choose, nothing will disappoint.

Food 8, Service 9, Atmosphere 9

 Jonah's *(right)*
Whale Beach
69 Bynya Road, Whale Beach
Tel: 02 9974 5599
www.jonahs.com.au
Open: daily, 8–10am, noon–3 pm

and 6.30–9pm
AU$250   *Modern Australian*

Perched on its clifftop throne overlooking the dreamy blue vista of the Pacific Ocean, Jonah's is one of Sydney's most exclusive boutique hotels and restaurants, found in one of the city's most elite residential areas. It's at least an hour's slog to drive from the city centre, but Jonah's regulars like to arrive in style, jetting in on a 12-minute seaplane from Rose Bay and landing in rockstar fashion where they are swiftly transferred to Jonah's by the hotel car. Start with a cocktail or a bottle from the 2,500-strong vintage wine list and head outside to the terrazzo. The breathtaking views are the same from the restaurant; with its floor-to-ceiling windows, it's near impossible to tear your eyes away from the epic panorama, especially on a summer's evening when the ocean is basked in a peachy glow. Now to the food. Chef George Fransisco's cuisine has consistently wooed the critics; it's both epic and fabulously hedonistic. Ask to be seated in one of the high-backed, creamy leather booths that hold court over the

rest of the tables and order the foie gras, a sweet starter eaten with mouthfuls of miniature buttermilk pancakes and served with prune and Armagnac ice cream. Also try the buttery spanner crab served in a sea urchin shell and follow with Hervey Bay scallops or aged, grain-fed entrecôte of beef (served for two), though take your time sharing the Grand Marnier mousse. Once you finish the last spoonful, you will be genuinely sorry to leave – that we can guarantee.

Food 9, Service 9, Atmosphere 7

LL Wine Dine (top)
42 Llankelly Place, Potts Point
Tel: 02 9356 8393
www.llwineanddine.com.au
Open: 4pm (10am Sat)–11pm
(midnight Thurs–Sat).
AU$80 **Modern Asian**

Once an illegal casino in the 1960s, then a swingers' club and even an adult bookshop named Ecstasy, this buzzy, Hong Kong-style eats 'n' drinks den sits in a pedestrian-only laneway in Sydney's former seedy red light district. While the neighbourhood has since flourished into a hipster haunt, the clever trio of brothers who own it aren't in hurry to forget its roots. Instead of binning a stash of vintage porn magazines they discovered during renovations, they created a tasteful collage of scantily-clad minxes on one of the walls. With red banquettes and oriental, dark-wood interiors, drinkers prop themselves up at the narrow bar for cocktails like Big Trouble in Little China (42 Below Vodka, coriander, pineap-

ple and vanilla) and linger for creative Asian cuisine in the front dining room or cosy rear, where seating is arranged in intimate nooks and over a split-level. LL's Sunday dumplings and cocktail jugs are sure-fire crowd-pleasers. So is the signature dish – Mao's pork belly buns, which disappear far too quickly between sharing friends. Order widely and order plenty. It's all good stuff – like black tea and star anise-smoked duck breast, crispy tofu with tahini and black sesame sauce and the old favourite – *san choi bow* with spicy lemongrass, lime and crunchy croutons.

Food 8, Service 9, Atmosphere 8

Longrain (bottom)
85 Commonwealth Street,
Surry Hills
Tel: 02 9280 2888
www.longrain.com
Open: noon–2.30pm Fri only,
daily, 4pm–midnight
AU$90 **Thai**

Longrain was a doyen in the modern Thai restaurant scene, and though a flurry of new openings has stolen some of the clientele, it remains a favourite of the Surry Hills set – schmoozing media types, graphic designers et al – who sup on Thai food to the backdrop of sexy lounge tunes spun by resident DJs. If you like what you hear, you can even pick up a copy of the CD – just ask the waitstaff to grab you one. Set in a spacious, converted warehouse, Longrain caters to Thai-loving gluttons as much as discerning cocktail-swillers; a highlight is the Bloody Mary, which has cult status among bartenders. If

you don't know what to order, simply ask the bartender or sommelier to pair something to complement your meal. All the cocktails and wines are designed with Martin Boetz's seasonal Thai cuisine in mind – he's a stickler for fresh ingredients. A kingfish curry with ginger, snake beans and lime leaves washes down marvellously with Stickmata, Longrain's signature cocktail with Sloeberry Vodka, strawberries, raspberries and blueberries, in case you need inspiration. The recently-opened Shortgrain, a Thai canteen and store, now shares the downstairs space.

Food 7, Service 8, Atmosphere 8

■ **Lotus** *(left)*
22 Challis Avenue, Potts Point
Tel: 02 9326 9000
www.merivale.com
Open: 6–10pm (11pm Fri / Sat) Tues–Sat
AU$120 **European / Asian**

As far as neighbourhood bistros go, Lotus is one of the better ones – largely down to its fabulous cocktails. Pair your meal with one or two of these babies and we're talking razzle-dazzle. In fact, it's a great idea to get there a little early and wedge yourself into the tiny adjacent bar area. With stunning Florence Broadhurst wallpaper and a striking back-lit bar, barmen mix up superb classics and punches (for two and four people) and around 16 wines by the glass. Venture into the restaurant

next door when you've worked up an appetite for chef Dan Hong's menu, and share plates of European cuisine spiked with delicate lacings of Asian influences, like scallop and duck ham washed in soy and pork belly with shiitake mushrooms and green garlic or fish of the day with silken tofu, mushrooms and kim chi consommé. Along with a sommelier, Lotus also offers food- and cocktail-matching. Try the Hemmetini, a refreshing pisco, mint and watermelon concoction paired with caramelised pork belly, goat's curd and watermelon.

Food 8, Service 8, Atmosphere 8

Manly Pavilion *(right)*
West Esplanade, Manly
Tel: 02 9949 9011
www.manlypavilion.com.au
Open: daily, noon–3pm, 6–10pm
AU$150   Contemporary / Italian

Travelling across to Manly for a meal used to elicit groans from Sydney's discerning eastside diners, but when the Manly Pavilion opened it didn't seem such a chore anymore. There was much hubbub among the foodies, too, when this restored pavilion reopened to the public in 2010 offering top-notch Mediterranean fare by acclaimed chef Jonathan Barthelmess and achingly beautiful harbourside views to boot. The glitzy surrounds will reflect on your bill, though Squillace Nicholas

Architects has done a Cinderella job on what was technically an 1930s bathers' dressing room, transforming the site into a glam harbourfront hotspot, with a light and breezy 150-seat split-level dining room that spills out through concertina doors onto a terrazzo balcony overlooking the water. Along with a 348-strong (and counting) wine list, the menu features light Italian style-fare. Start with freshly-shucked oysters, sliver thin slices of sashimi and move on to scampi, celery ragu with *bagna càuda* and mains from the *carne, pesce* or pasta menus. Carnivores will be lost for words when they smother their succulent piece of 12-hour braised beef short rib with rich, luscious bone marrow. Heavy, hedonistic stuff.

Food 8, Service 7, Atmosphere 9

 Manta *(top)*
6 Cowper Wharf Road,
Woolloomooloo
Tel: 02 9332 3822
www.mantarestaurant.com.au
Open: daily, noon–3pm, 6–10pm
AU$120 **Seafood**

Manta is one of the swankier spots in Sydney to sit on the waterfront, slurping down freshly-shucked oysters and looking suitably smug. This contemporary seafood restaurant spills out al fresco onto Woolloomooloo's Finger Wharf and with crisp, white tablecloths and gleaming multimillion-dollar yachts mere metres away, the menu showcases some of the best examples of Australia's so-fresh-it's-still-wiggling seafood. The grilled whole Yamba king prawns, doused in a buttery sauce of

parsley, garlic and olive oil, are almost too good to share, so order by the kilo. The seafood *bouillabaisse*, however, must be shared – stuffed with a hearty selection of seafood like king prawns, Alaskan king crab, Atlantic scallops, hiramasa kingfish, clams, black mussels and Clarence River calamari, it's designed for two, and easy to see why. Manta might be seafood-heavy, but meat aficionados aren't ignored with plenty of carnivorous items to choose from like grass-fed black Angus fillet, dry-aged for six weeks. If you're early, bag yourself one of the comfy banquettes and order something from sommelier Lyndon Stenning's wine list.

Food 8, Service 8, Atmosphere 8

 Marque *(bottom)*
4/5 355 Crown Street, Surry Hills
Tel: 02 9332 2225
www.marquerestaurant.com.au
Open: noon–3pm Fri only,
6.30–11pm Mon–Sat
AU$300 **Modern Australian**

Chefs Mark Best and Pasi Petanen are masters of calculated culinary risk, creating such an exquisite degustation menu it would silence even the most cynical critic. Each course is so beautifully presented and so remarkably flawless in texture, taste and appearance the restaurant deservedly took home the 'Best Restaurant' title in the Sydney Good Food awards. From delicate almond jelly with chunks of blue swimmer crab, spatchcock with shallots, leek, white asparagus and ox heart, or a magnificent chocolate mousse 'écrasé', with eucalyptus and coconut, take

a seat in the smart black-lacquered, dark-wood and white-clothed dining room and expect the best in food, service and wine, without the pomp plaguing other restaurants of this calibre. Be sure to choose the degustation, with matching wines from sommeliers Nicolas André and Zoltan Magyar, who swan around advising diners on what to pair with what. Whether it's a risotto of South Australian calamari and prawn or a warm chocolate ganache with praline, lemongrass and rosemary, they're always on the money.

Food 10, Service 9, Atmosphere 7

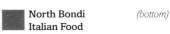

Monkey Magic *(top)*
3&4/410 Crown Street, Surry Hills
Tel: 02 9358 4444
www.monkeymagic.com.au
Open: 6–10pm. Closed Sundays.
AU$80   ***Japanese***

A firm favourite with local hipsters, this sexy, warehouse-style space, on the upper level above Crown Street, is abuzz with diners, chattering at cosy tables lit by flickering candles. The vibe is slick, cool and urban, and it's all about high-quality fish and traditional Japanese with New York pizzazz. Start with a few cocktails and order dishes to share – head chef Hidetoshi Tsuboi is a master of preparing artfully-presented dishes that tend to disappear quickly – like succulent morsels of crab and zingy pickled daikon resting on betel leaf. Sushi master Michiaki Miyazaki cut his teeth working at two-Michelin-starred restaurant Kikuoni in Kyoto, Japan, joining the kitchen at 18 only to become head chef a decade

later, meaning you can't go wrong with an assorted sashimi or sushi plate (each piece served with its own unique sauce). Other stand-outs are the soft shell crab roll served with fried leek and zesty wasabi mayonnaise and the toothfish, with a light, feathery texture and baked with a buttery miso sauce, served with pink grapefruit salad dowsed with harissa dressing.

Food 7, Service 7, Atmosphere 8

North Bondi *(bottom)*
Italian Food
118-120 Ramsgate Avenue, Bondi Beach
Tel: 02 9300 4400
www.idrb.com
Open: daily, 6pm (noon Fri–Sun)
–midnight
AU$80   ***Italian***

Overlooking Sydney's famous Bondi beach, with record and rock band posters plastered over the walls and ceilings, Maurice Terzini's Italian eatery is about as hip as it gets in Sydney. It's a favourite of the achingly cool Bondi crowd and their permanently bronzed limbs, Ksubi jeans and rakish porkpie hats. On a summer's afternoon, nothing quite beats shelling peanuts and sipping Campari mixed with freshly-squeezed blood orange juice after an ocean dip, but you may be forced to guzzle several if you want stay on and eat a meal. Infuriatingly, NBIF doesn't take bookings and the place is perennially packed with locals. If you do manage to woo one of the waiters, hip young things in denim aprons, you have hit the jackpot. Expect classic Italian antipasti for sharing, like Italian sardines served in the tin with crunchy, chargrilled bruschetta, crisp-yet-tender calamari, veal scaloppini, pizza and pasta.

Food 8, Service 7, Atmosphere 9

Neutral Bay *(left)*
Bar & Dining
132 Military Road, Neutral Bay
Tel: 02 9953 5853
www.nbbaranddining.com.au
Open: 5pm (noon Fri–Sun)–10.30pm
(10pm Sun). Closed Mon & Tues.
AU$80 ***Modern Australian***

Perched on busy Military Road with its high ceilings, long benches and tawny-coloured high-backed booths, the NBBD is a classy diner. It's inevitably busy most nights with hip northern suburb locals who couldn't believe their luck when owner Alex Kearns decided to open a second well-priced sister restaurant to Glebe Point Diner (407 Glebe Point Road, tel: 02 9660 2646). The staff are young, fresh and professional, with waiters eager to relay the classic modern Australian/Mediterranean menu. It's peppered with great dishes, from Tasmanian Pacific and Pambula rock oysters, to skewers of kingfish and pork belly with tarragon salsa, and an expertly-made 240-gram grass-fed Coorong Angus Scotch fillet, smeared with horseradish. Drinks-wise, there are some tasty cocktails on the menu and wine-lovers are well catered to, and a decent bottle won't cost an arm or a leg, either.

Food 8, Service 9, Atmosphere 8

Ocean Room   *(right)*
Ground Level, Overseas Passenger
Terminal, Circular Quay West, The Rocks
Tel: 02 9252 9585
www.oceanroomsydney.com
Open: noon–2pm Tues–Fri, 6–10pm
(midnight Fri/Sat) Mon–Sat
AU$170   *Japanese*

Perched on a wharf opposite the gleaming white sails of the Opera House, the Ocean Room has one of Sydney's most enviable views, either from the outdoor tables on the wharf, or from the interior dining room. However, if there happens to be a large P&O cruiser in town, you'll munch on your sushi gazing straight through a porthole. Should that happen, it won't detract from the knockout Yasumich Morita-designed dining room, resplendent with its timber ceiling art, and certainly not from the masterful Japanese cuisine created by chef Raita Noda. The seafood is sensational and the artful, delicate degustation tasting menu is a journey in every sense of the word. It starts with fresh rock oysters and peaks with Tuna Creation, the house speciality of five slices of fish served five ways: oil-blanched, raw, seared, fresh raw or marinated. Each comes with a tiny sprinkling of seasoning and condiment to highlight texture and taste; the seared slice, for example, is paired with soy salt aged for three years, five peppers and zesty baubles of salmon roe. Don't miss out on the cocktails, either; seven creations based on the seven Japanese gods of fortune.

Food 8, Service 9, Atmosphere 8

eat...

Otto Ristorante *(left)*
Area 8/6 Cowper Wharf Road, Woolloomooloo
Tel: 02 9368 7488
www.ottoristorante.com.au
Open: daily, noon–10.30pm
AU$300   **Italian**

The who's who of Sydney flocks to Otto, a leading light in the fine-dining world, with Chef Richard Ptacnik's Italian menu as well turned out as the designer bag-toting regulars. The setting isn't too shabby, either – think white-clothed tables spilling out onto the wooden Finger Wharf, overlooking a flotilla of gleaming white yachts and cashed-up clientele. Look out for Russell Crowe – he's a regular. From cured meats like prosciutto, *capocollo*, spicy salami, bresaola and *ciccioli* served with *muscatels* and rockmelon mustard to thinly-sliced pink snapper with salsa verde, peas and fresh, aromatic herbs, or perhaps a decadent 650-gram crayfish spaghetti doused in brandy, napolitana sauce, cherry tomatoes and baby basil – order with confidence. Service is doting and all dishes are served with classic Italian finesse, even through the chef hails from Prague. It's one of those restaurants to head to if you feel like a stand-out, no-holds (or expenses) barred meal.

Food 9, Service 9, Atmosphere 8

Pendolino *(middle)*
Level 2, The Strand Arcade,
412-414 George Street, CBD
Tel: 02 9231 6117
www.pendolino.com.au
Open: noon–3pm, 6–10pm.
Closed Sundays.
AU$150   **Italian**

It might seem an unlikely locale, perched atop an upper level of Sydney's high-brow, historic shopping arcade The Strand, but Pendolino is one of Sydney's favourite Italian restaurants. Atmospheric and quintessentially Italian, it's ideal for a romantic dinner as it's so dimly-lit the white apron-clad waitstaff will bring you a pen torch to read the menu. Fans of drizzling will fall in love with Chef Nino Zoccali's exper-

tise on all things olive oil – he is an aficionado and various drops are poured generously over handmade flour and organic egg pasta and other wonderful ingredients, like bursting-with-flavour heirloom tomatoes or buffalo mozzarella. From hand-cut pappardelle and veal ragu or rare-seared herb and garlic-crusted South Coast yellow fin tuna, this is Italian fare at its finest, and should you fall in love with the good oil, simply head over to the next door boutique, Lolioteca, which stocks vinegar, olives and more Tuscan and Umbrian extra virgins than the Vatican.

Food 8, Service 9, Atmosphere 8

Pilu *(right)*
Freshwater Beach, end
of Moore Road, Freshwater
Tel: 02 9938 3331
www.piluatfreshwater.com.au
Open: noon–2.30pm, 6–9.30pm. Closed
Sunday evening and Mondays.
AU$150   Italian (Sardinian)

When Sydney turns it on with a blisteringly beautiful, blue-sky summer's day, there are few better places in the world to be than at Pilu. Giovanni Pilu's beach house restaurant overlooks one of the favourite northern beaches known as Freshwater (or Freshie, to the locals), and what better way to soak up the salty air and the vista of breaking waves than with seafood? Battered fish fillets, calamari and prawns can be bought at any corner fish shop, but at Pilu you might have to restrain the urge to shove as many in your mouth as you can. Other Sardinian seafood delights include grilled scampi, oven-baked whole baby snapper with *vernaccia* and green olives, hand-made egg pasta ravioli, meat dishes and fresh tomato and basil salad. With floor-to-ceiling windows that offer one of the best beachy views in Sydney, there's nothing pompous about the place, though the relaxed service can teeter on the edge of too relaxed at times. Must be all the salt in the air.

Food 8, Service 6, Atmosphere 9

Pizza e Birra *(top)*
500 Crown Street, Surry Hills
Tel: 02 9332 2510
www.pizzabirra.com.au
Open: daily, noon (5.30pm Mon–Weds)
–11pm (Thurs–Sat)
AU$60   **Pizza**

If you're hankering for pizza, this is one of Sydney's best. The thin-crusted bases with chunky toppings, strands of chewy mozzarella and fresh herbs make the pizza here outrageously popular, and the location, right on the perennially hip, hubbub of Crown Street, helps, too. Fronting onto the street, with a couple of tables on the footpath outside, the restaurant is only a few steps away from some other Crown Street offerings: The Clock pub and Mille Vini, an Italian wine bar owned by the same owners. As for the pizza, the wood-fired oven thin crusts means it's perfectly acceptable to munch down an entire one to yourself – you won't want to share it, that's for sure. From simple margherita with tomato, buffalo mozzarella, basil and parmesan, expect little twists, such as truffle oil drizzled over the Speck pizza, an enticing mix of potatoes, mozzarella, provola, speck and parmesan. Beer-lovers will be in their element here, as the birra at Pizza e Birra tends to be sourced from eclectic boutique breweries around Australia – ask the waiters what's new.

Food 8, Service 8, Atmosphere 8

Porteño *(bottom)*
58 Cleveland Street, Surry Hills
Tel: 02 8399 1440
www.porteno.com.au
Open: noon–3pm Sun, 6–11pm Tues–Sat
AU$140   **Argentinean**

One of the most exciting spots to open in Sydney of late, Porteño is an Argentinean grillhouse in an incredible Spanish-style villa, complete with white-washed walls, a courtyard and wrought iron railings. Its trend-setting, tattooed chef/owners Elvis Abrahanowicz and Ben Milgate also own Bodega (see page 78), and after introducing Sydney to tapas done the way it should be done, they've moved onto succulent meats, cooked *asador*-style. It's dinner and a show here, as carcasses meet their flamey death over a fruitwood fire, crucified on a metal brace. Carve up some Victorian Suffolk lamb shin, six-hour cooked suckling pig, and slice it up on your chopping board, with lashings of piquant *chimichurri* sauce. Let the rockabilly-dressed hostess, Sarah Doyle, or the waitstaff recommend other tapas-style dishes to share. Upstairs there's another bar and a moody lounge area, with antique foosball tables, sumptuous Chesterfields and paintings of Eva Perón. You could easily spend a night up here with a group of friends or having an intimate tête-à-tête with a foxy date. Estella is on tap and stellar cocktails like the Palermo Hollywood with tequila, apple juice, vanilla, sage and cinnamon pack a potent punch. For pudding, don't forgo Porteño's Argentina-meets-Australia mango pavlova, smothered in the sinfully sweet

South American dulce de leche and a smattering of peanuts.

Food 9 Service 8 Atmosphere 10

Public Dining Room *(left)*
2A The Esplanade, Balmoral Beach
Tel: 02 9968 4880
www.publicdiningroom.com.au
Open: daily, noon (8am Sat/ Sun)–10pm (10.30pm Sat/Sun)
AU$80   Modern Mediterranean

With breezy, blonde hardwood floors white marble bar and floor-to-ceiling glass doors overlooking Balmoral Beach, Public Dining Room is hard to beat for a long, leisurely lunch in summer. The seagulls, sand and sunlight streaming through the doors, fig trees growing outside and the decked terrace makes it feels like the ultimate beach house (the one we all want to live in). If only Chef Nick Raitt could be our personal cook, too. The light, fresh Mediterranean menu that begins with oysters from a Batemen's Bay oysterage – if you're lucky the four-year-old oysters won't have sold out, but the *Clair de Lune* are a good bet. They've been exposed to choppy sea conditions, apparently, and are akin to a wave crashing on your tongue. Raitt also loves his purées, which are scattered throughout the menu, in starters like the roasted scallop with pickled fungi (Jerusalem artichoke purée) and in main courses like tender fillet steak

on a bed of puy lentils, king brown mushroom and porcini butter (roast pumpkin purée). Be sure to let the attentive wait staff recommend a drop from the wine library.

Food 8, Service 8, Atmosphere 8

 **Riverview** *(right)*
Hotel & Dining
29 Birchgrove Road, Balmain
Tel: 02 9810 1151
www.theriverviewhotel.com.au
Open: daily, noon–3pm, 6–10pm
AU$60 *Modern British*

When the British coined the term gastropub, Australian pub-owners scoffed. Replace humble meat pie and mash with fancy fine-dining? It seemed ludicrous, and many would argue it to the grave. Until they dined at the Riverview. This is one classy pub with some outstanding grub. Built in the 1880s, the 'Riv', as it's known to Balmain locals, has all the cosiness and welcoming vibe of a pub, but with the food of a well-heeled restaurant. It's a brilliant spot for a Sunday afternoon drink and lunch, with not a white tablecloth in sight. Choose from a menu that celebrates the best of contemporary British fare with Chef Brad Sloane's olive-crusted lamb rump with globe artichoke and gently-warmed feta, handmade pasta, and roast duck breast already winning a number of foodie gongs, including Gastronomic Hotel of the Year. If you just want to down some ice-cold schooners and have a nibble, there's a great tasting plate for two featuring succulent prawn and chorizo brochettes, crab and whitebait *fritto* and potted Wagyu *en croûte*. You'll never want to go to an average pub again.

Food 8, Service 7, Atmosphere 8

Rockpool Bar & Grill   *(left)*
66 Hunter Street, The Rocks
Tel: 02 8078 1900
www.rockpool.com.au
Open: noon–3pm, 6–11pm. Closed
Sat lunch and Sundays.
AU$250   **Steakhouse**

Set inside the glamorous, 1936 Emil Sodersten-designed building, this is one of Sydney's finest Art Deco masterpieces, so it's only fitting that after a AU$35-million investment it became home to one of Sydney's finest restaurants. With its magnificent green marble columns, soaring vaulted ceilings, dark leather décor and bustling open kitchen, walking inside is a feast for the eyes, though rest assured all the other senses get a work out, too. Celebrity chef Neil Perry is the darling of the foodie world for good reason – he is obsessive over fine details and all produce is sustainably-farmed and treated humanely. From grain to grass-fed, Perry sources only the best beef from Australia like Blackmore's Wagyu, Greenhams and Rangers Valley. It's then dried on-site and cooked over the wood-fire (the seafood in the charcoal grill) to perfection – try the sizeable rib-eye cooked minute-style. Sides are just as epic; just one spoonful and you may want to smother yourself instead of your Blackmore 220-gram wagyu in creamed corn,

mushy peas with a slow-cooked egg or mac and cheese. As for the liquids, the spectacular wine list extends to frighteningly-priced bottles worth several tens of thousands of dollars, while over at the stunning bar are Australia's finest cocktail barmen, mixing up flawless old-school classics. It all costs a pretty penny, but dining doesn't get much better than this.

Food 10, Service 9, Atmosphere 9

Rockpool *(right)*
107 George Street, The Rocks
Tel: 02 9252 1888
www.rockpool.com.au
Open: 6–11pm Tues-Sat
AU$350   Contemporary/Seafood

The original trailblazer in chef Neil Perry's slew of Australian restaurants,

Rockpool is a classy restaurant that has been consistently delivering a solid, superior culinary experience for more than 21 years. The 110-seat restaurant might have aged gracefully, but the interiors were given a nip and tuck in 2007, with sturdy leather banquettes and white-linen tablecloths, sleek wooden ramp and photographic murals by Earl Carter and David Band. Under Perry's watchful eye, the restaurant has aged extremely well and functions like a well-oiled machine. From the re-filling of bread and topping-up of mineral water, to thoughtful wine pairings, there are few restaurants in Sydney with such flawless service. Perry is one of Australia's best-known celebrity chefs and his fanaticism for fresh, fine produce means you could bet your last dollar on your mother that each and every one of the five- or eight-courses in the grand tasting menu will be wickedly

delicious, like the supple squid ceviche with bacon, lime and coriander, or slow-roasted farm lamb with heirloom carrots, Medjool dates and carrot soufflé. All the seafood is sustainable, too, meaning you can guzzle it down with a clear conscience – particularly the sustainable shark fin soup, made sans shark.

Food 9, Service 9, Atmosphere 8

███ **Rosso Pomodoro** *(left)*
      24 Buchanan Street, Balmain
Tel: 02 9555 5924
www.rossopomodoro.com.au
Open: 6–10pm. Closed Mondays.
AU$60   *Pizza*

Set in the quiet area known as White Bay, you would not be surprised to see a tumbleweed scampering past around this neck of the woods, but pizza aficionados will travel – especially for the crusty, thin-based pizza at Rosso Pomodoro. This is an unassuming little restaurant tucked beneath some apartments, and as it's a hefty walk from the main pub 'n' eats area of Balmain, it's best to drive or take a taxi. Its odd location doesn't seem to bother the locals, though, who crowd in on any given night of the week for Italian-style pizza, cooked expertly with some strict rules like 'No half and half'. The specials are chalked up on the board and there are a few large round tables ideal for a group of friends. Moreish creations abound, but the stand-out has to be the Rocco, laden with fresh tomato, mozzarella,

rocket, prosciutto and shaved parmesan. There's no corkage, either, so bring along that vino. Our only quibble is the toilet – it's a hike away.

Food 8, Service 7, Atmosphere 8

Sailors Thai *(right)*
106 George Street, The Rocks
Tel: 02 9251 2466
www.sailorsthai.com.au
Open: noon–2.30pm, 6–10pm. Closed Sat lunch and Sundays.
AU$80 *Thai*

Most Aussies will proclaim loudly that Australia does Thai better than Thailand, and after eating at Sailors Thai, you might be inclined to agree. There are two other venues in Potts Point and in the Ivy bar megacomplex (330 George Street, tel: 02 9240 3000), but this atmospheric sandstone restaurant in The Rocks is the original, with a chic restaurant downstairs and a laid-back, much-loved street food-style canteen complete with communal tables upstairs. If you had to choose one dish to eat and die happy, it would be Sailors' fat, juicy Yamba prawns served in crunchy betel leaves and sprinkled with chilli, peanut and lime. Elsewhere on the menu, beef salads, duck curry or caramelised pork chops never fail to send tastebuds into a tizzy, each made with a careful blend of the tangy, pungent herbs and spices that make Thai food such a culinary treat.

Food 9, Service 7, Atmosphere 8

Sake *(top)*
12 Argyle Street, The Rocks
Tel: 02 9259 5656
www.sakerestaurant.com.au
Open: noon–3pm, 6–10.30pm (midnight Fri/Sat). Closed Sat/Sun lunch.
AU$90 *Japanese*

Lively, fun and Nippon-trendy, Sake's wall of brightly-coloured sake barrels, cherry blossom wallpaper and abuzz tatami dining area make for a frolicsome night out with a group of friends rather than an intimate dinner for two; although it suits anyone searching for Japan's elusive *umami*, particularly with sushi guru Shaun Presland at the helm. After slicing sashimi for Sushi e at the Establishment, Presland was poached by Nobu Matsihusa to open Nobu Atlantis in the Bahamas, and it's easy to see why he's a darling of the foodie world. Presland is a master at his craft, and the menu is a testament to his background of learning the ins and outs of the cuisine at a 350-year-old traditional wooden inn in Japan. Sit at the sushi counter to watch his nimble nigiri and sashimi skills. Everything tastes exemplary, though it's worth venturing beyond sushi to Presland's tartare trio of salmon, tuna and kingfish, devilishly tender pork belly or miso cuttlefish, grilled to perfection and marinated in sweet miso sauce. The name might be a hint, but don't forget to drink and dine – along with 14 sake and shochu cocktails, the bar is most famous for its Kozaemon sakes, which are exclusively sourced from the 300-year-old Nakashima brewery in Japan, served chilled or warmed for AU$3-6 per tasting glass.

Food 8 Service 8 Atmosphere 9

 Spice I Am *(bottom)*
Shop 1, 90 Wentworth Avenue, Surry Hills
Tel: 02 9280 0928
www.spiceiam.com
Open: 11.30am–3pm, 6–10pm. Closed Mondays.
AU$50 *Thai*

The best beef massamam in the world – better than the beef massamam in Thailand. Impossible, you say? Then check out the queues outside this tiny Thai eatery. They spill out onto the street, with hopeful diners tapping their feet impatiently and staring hungrily at the clatter of steaming plates being passed around heaped with succulent pork belly, Thai beef salad and the famous beef massaman. But wait, there are more people waiting in the pub around the corner, having given their mobile numbers to the busy, but friendly waitstaff. There's a reason they queue, and it's not just because there are no bookings – it's for outstanding Thai food at cheap-as-chips prices. There are few better places serving such quality Thai, imbued with fragrant herbs and spices, and even fewer where you can hand over a AU$50 and still have change for the taxi ride home. So successful is this little joint, the owners went and opened a swanky sister venue in Darlinghurst (296-300 Victoria Street, tel: 02 9332 2445) and another one around the corner in Surry Hills (202 Elizabeth Street, tel: 02 9280 0364). But at twice the price, it's got nothing on the original. Aside from the beef massamam, and usual curry sus

suspects, order the Thai Som Tum – green papaya, chopped up chilli, peanuts, shrimp and tangy dressing of lime and fish sauce. And feel free to bring a bottle – there's no corkage.

Food 9, Service 7, Atmosphere 8

Spice Temple *(top)*
10 Bligh Street, CBD
Tel: 02 8078 1888
www.rockpool.com.au
Open: noon–3pm, 6–10pm (11pm Fri/Sat). Closed Sat lunch and Sundays.
AU$150 *Chinese*

Owned by Australian celebrity chef Neil Perry, this slinky Asian restaurant is a glamorous hotspot and its dimly-lit, scarlet-coloured dining room is the high temple of regional Chinese cuisine. From spicy Sichuan to fiery Hunan, most dishes pack a chilli punch and many even require on-site murder – live mud crabs or clams are ordered by request from the tank (superb with an aromatic duck salad imbued with coriander or Yunnan-style shiitake, oyster, enoki and wild Chinese mushrooms) while leatherjacket is 'drowned' in a sauce of fire-breathing piquancy. Not a spice lover? Don't panic – not everything has a spice kick and all the dishes that do come highlighted in red on the menu, so there will be no unwelcome surprises. You can always cool off with a refreshing Asian-inspired cocktail, based on the twelve Zodiac signs of the Chinese calendar – like the zesty Rooster, orange with Aperol, Limoncello and passionfruit. Some dishes, like the Sichuan-influenced 'eight treasure boned whole

duck' require 24-hours notice, so book ahead if you're in feasting mode.

Food 8, Service 8, Atmosphere 9

Sushi e *(bottom)*
Level 4, Establishment Hotel, 252 George Street, CBD
www.merivale.com
Tel: 02 9240 3000
Open: noon–3pm, 6pm (6.30pm Fri/Sat)–10.30pm. Closed Sat lunch and Sun.
AU$120 *Sushi / Japanese*

Sushi-e was one of the first Sydney restaurants to jump on the Nobu bandwagon, and has wooed the city's glossy-maned, Manolo-wearing socialites and city bankers ever since. Its success also had a helpful nudge thanks to the fact it's on the same level as Hemmesphere, one of the city's sexiest cocktail bars. Set on the upper-level of the Establishment building, you need to walk through its Moorish opulence to reach Sushi-e, and simply wander back after your meal for a nightcap (it would be rude not to). Slicing seafood with agile fingers and skilled mastery, chef Nobuyuki Ura and his team work their magic behind a central counter – there are only around 25 seats at the counter so make sure to call ahead so you can ogle while they create edible art. All the standard classics are present and correct, like freshest-of-fresh kingfish slices lightly fused with citrus-imbued soy sauce (ponzu) and the complete selection of nigiri sushi. If you're more than peckish, larger dishes like 500-day grain-fed Wagyu beef or miso-swathed cod are here, too. The crowd favourite? The selection of eight porcelain tasting

spoons – perfect if you're dining a deux with two servings of sublime Japanese appetisers.

Food 9, Service 8, Atmosphere 9

Table for 20 *(left)*
82 Campbell Street, Surry Hills
Tel: 02 4160 96916
www.tablefor20.blogspot.com
Open: dinner 8pm, Wed–Fri
AU$60   *Italian*

Part-dinner party, part-guerrilla dining, Table for 20 is one of Sydney's most clandestine and intimate dining experiences, but hop to it if you want to try it, because like the name suggests, there are only 20 spaces for bums on seats. Set in a converted warehouse with lots of exposed brick walls and flickering candlelight, dining here is a chic, one-of-a-kind experience that evolved

naturally from owner Michael Fantuz's love of throwing dinner parties for his friends. The three-course set menu is wholesome, hearty Italian fare and while groups tend to book out the restaurant, which has one massive communal table, individual reservations are also common and the vibe is convivial and warm. The best part is you never know who you might sit next to, and unlike other restaurants, striking up a friendly conversation with the stranger sitting next to you is welcome. Either bring your own bottle or order from the menu; either way, the wine flows as freely as the chat. An eclectic and incredibly enjoyable community dining experience – don't forget to head upstairs to Sticky for some cocktails, a fantastic, equally intimate bar also owned by Fantuz.

Food 7, Service 8, Atmosphere 9

eat...

Tetsuya's *(right)*
529 Kent Street, CBD
Tel: 02 9267 2900
www.tetsuyas.com
Open: noon–2.30pm Sat, 6–9.30pm
Tues–Sat
AU$500 ***French/Japanese***

The affable, world-class chef Tetsuya Wakuda (known affectionately as 'Tets' to most Aussies) is lauded by foodies around the globe, winning every imaginable gong and accolade under the sun for his meticulously-crafted cuisine, which combines Japanese inspiration with classic French techniques. His Sydney restaurant is rightfully considered one the country's best (if not *the* best), and it can take months to secure a reservation, so you'll need to plan well in advance if you want any hope of eating there. With floor-to-ceiling windows facing delicate Japanese gardens, the restaurant is a subdued, elegant ryokan style with its damask tablecloths setting the scene for a culinary experience few chefs could hope to rival. Beginning with a flute of Bollinger, the 12- or 14-course degustation moves from small, perfectly-formed dish to the next, small, perfectly-formed dish, and while every mouthful will live on in your memory, his confit of ocean trout, on a bed of apple, konbu and celery is globally-renowned. It might be because the Japanese-born chef's love affair with food extends far beyond what might be deemed normal, but he's a master at sourcing flawless produce and is a long-standing friend of the owners of Petuna Seafood, who farm some of the country's premier seafood in the choppy waters of Tasmania's southwest wilderness. Memorable, epic, and one for a special occasion.

Food 9, Service 9, Atmosphere 8

Toko *(left)*

490 Crown Street, Surry Hills
Tel: 02 9357 6100
www.toko.com.au
Open: noon–3pm Tues–Fri,
6–11pm Mon–Sat

AU$90   *Japanese*

With its honey-coloured timber interiors, sumptuous leather banquettes and the cream of Sydney's fashion crop nibbling on dainty bites of sashimi, Toko is the cool kid in Surry Hills, but the expertly executed Japanese cuisine deserves a nod, too. The finely-sliced ocean trout and snapper sashimi is always of the melt-in-the-mouth variety, while anything off the chargrilled *robata* grill smells, looks and tastes exceptional. If you think Japanese is done

and dusted, Toko may surprise you. There's nothing overtly radical on the menu but the pairings are unique – like duck breast with nashi pear, or the divine miso-marinated lamb cutlets. Best to dust off something decent to wear, because Toko is a place to be seen, too, and on any given night the place is packed and the atmosphere is buzzy. The counter will give you the chance to watch the slicing and dicing chefs, but you can opt to sit in one of the street-level tables if you want to bask in the jealous stares from passers-by strolling along Crown Street.

Food 8, Service 8, Atmosphere 9

Tomislav *(right)*
2/13 Kirketon Road, Darlinghurst
Tel: 02 9356 4535
www.tomislav.com.au
Open: noon–3pm Fri, 6–10pm Tues–Sat
AU$150 ***Modern Australian***

Chef Tomislav Martinovic comes from good culinary stock – he worked in Heston Blumenthal's kitchen and wows patrons with his own molecular pizzazz at his eponymous restaurant, starting with the feather-thin rice crackers or thrice-cooked, hand-cut chips that are spritzed with a DIY atomiser bottle of vinegar. Set on an upper terrace overlooking William Street and the neon glow of the King's Cross Coca-Cola sign, this is a bistro with no airs or graces – it's brilliant for a casual evening meal with expert, courteous waitstaff and an open-air kitchen that pumps out a small, thoughtful menu. All dishes feature local and regional produce, like slow-poached Comboyne Hen's Egg served with a smattering of peas and warm potato cream, roast Redgate quail or Hereford scotch fillet with roast bone marrow so succulent it could make even the most stiff-lipped gastronome weep. The desserts will bring out the child in everyone, especially the caramelised apple crumble tart, imbued with clotted ice-cream and a mouthful of tongue-fizzling popping candy – a memorable finish.

Food 8, Service 9, Atmosphere 7

Uccello   *(opposite)*
Level 4, Ivy Complex,
320-330 George Street, CBD
Tel: 02 9240 3000
www.merivale.com
Open: noon–3pm Tues–Fri, 1–5pm
Sun (summer only); 6–11pm Tues–Sat
AU$150   ***Italian***

This white and yellow, light and bustling Italian dining room in the megacomplex known as Ivy is fabulous to look at and better yet, it sits astride the hedonist's playground of the Ivy Pool Club, complete with buff lifeguards and 25-metre rooftop pool. It can be difficult to slurp up a strand of angel hair pasta when there are rippling six packs and cavorting babes in bikinis mere metres away, especially if you've snared one of the outdoor tables right next to the action, but if you tear your eyes away from the frolicking beautiful people, there's a fairly reputable Italian dining experience to enjoy. Settle in and order it all – from San Daniele prosciutto with buffalo mozzarella and antipasti. Pastafarians will go mad for the handmade pasta; try the squid-ink tagliolini for the primi, mains like roast baby organic chicken or pan-roasted fillet of coral trout for secondi. The epic dolci – if you can fit it in, that is – we'll leave up to you, though you're in safe hands choosing anything. Chef Eugenio Riva does a sterling job with handmade pasta and trattoria classics and best of all, spending your cash here pretty much guarantees you entrance to the wonderland pool club – notorious for its tough door policy.

Food 8, Service 8, Atmosphere 9

drink

Australians are famous for their love of beer-swilling and the pub is a cultural fixture. These days there are equally as many upmarket pubs fitted with marble and chrome, DJs and landscaped beer gardens as there are seedier inner-city joints with poker machines, footy screens and grizzled, old-timers propping up the bar. Whichever pub you happen across, one thing is guaranteed: a skilfully-poured, ice-cold beer, usually served in a schooner or smaller glasses – either a middy or a hybrid of the two, what's known as a schmiddy. The latest trend for many bars is beer served in a longneck or a 'longie', a large 750ml bottle of beer characterised by, you guessed it, a long neck. Forget about Fosters, though – no Sydneysider drinks it. Some standard local brews include VB (Victoria Bitter), Carlton or Tooheys, with Coopers Pale Ale, James Boags and Cascade classified as 'middle range'. As tastes have evolved and palates have become more discerning, Australian pub stocks have also gone upmarket. Even the dinkiest pub is more likely to put on a spread of artisanal lagers from boutique breweries, imported craft beers and low-carb offerings like Pure Blonde for gullible fitness freaks.

Pubs hit the spot for casual boozing, but when it comes to bars, Sydney's scene has always come a bitter second to Melbourne and its character-filled laneway drinkeries. For years, the process of opening a new bar was thwarted by prohibitive state licensing laws. Wannabe bar owners had to apply for a frighteningly expensive AU$15,000-a-year hotelier's licence, and as a result, the majority of the city's bars and pubs have been dominated by a few prominent hospitality families. The Hemmes family, in particular, own a bursting-at-the-seams portfolio of Sydney's bars – including the Miami-style wonderland of Ivy, with its numerous swanky cocktail and poolside bars.

Over the past few years, however, Sydney has undergone what's been dubbed the 'small bar revolution' thanks to Lord Mayor Clover Moore, who enacted legislation

in 2009 to make it easier for individuals to get a liquor licence – without forking out their life savings for the privilege.

Since then a slew of hip, hidey-hole bars have flourished, revitalising Sydney's drinking scene and reinvigorating many of the city's long-forgotten laneways. Many were launched by fashionable groups of twenty- or thirty-something mates, and as most of them are first-time bar-owners, it's injected some much-needed freshness into the scene. As the momentum gains steam, it seems not a week passes without news of yet another small, edgy bar opening in a once-disused urban lane. The best include Grasshopper, Sticky, Shady Pines Saloon and Pocket.

For cocktails, you're in expert hands. Sydney has a sophisticated scene on par with London and New York. For a deftly-mixed negroni or Old Fashioned we've listed the city's top-notch cocktail bars, manned by some talented, world-class mixol-ogists, particularly Eau de Vie, Zeta, Rockpool Bar & Grill and Hemmesphere. Sydneysiders are also extraordinarily savvy with regard to wine, with a slew of intimate places to swirl, slosh and quaff local and Euro drops. The best are Wine Library, Bambini Wine Room, Love Tilly Devine, Fico and Time to Vino.

Boozing indoors is all well and good, but with Sydney's climate and eye-candy harbour, locals have perfected the art of tippling al fresco. Most pubs will have beer gardens, and there are dozens of drinking spots where you can clink glasses and say 'cheers' while gazing at a devastating water view – try Opera Bar on the concourse of the Opera House for starters. Most others fit into the restaurant-bar category; for the most stylish food 'n' views drinkeries, flip to the Eat chapter and check out Icebergs, North Bondi Italian Food, Hugos Bar Pizza Manly, Manta and Firefly Wine & Tapas.

Absinthe Salon (left)
87 Albion Street, Surry Hills
Tel: 02 9211 6632
www.absinthesalon.com.au
Open: 4–10pm Weds–Sun

Poor old absinthe is as ostracised as the fat kid in high school. The mere mention of it might make you shudder at the hazy memory of flame-lit shots at the bar, but Absinthe Salon-owers Gaye Valttila and Joop van Heusden want to change all that. In a first for Sydney (and the world), they launched their miniscule Parisian-styled drinkery in 2010 to much acclaim. If you've ever wanted to know more about this remarkable drink, this stylish little bar, with its Gothic atmosphere and 19th-century flair, should be on your radar. Though you can forget about green fairies, because as certified absintheurs (you read it right), Joop and Gaye want to educate their clientele, and their first point of contention is the green haze – a gross exaggeration, apparently. The 26 absinthes are sampled by the traditional method of pouring water over a cube of sugar in a spoon resting on the glass. Water trickles from the vintage fountain taps at each table, dissolving the sugar into the glass to 'louche' (dilute) the absinthe. It's a fascinating process, but make sure to call ahead. The bar is a tiny slip of a thing, with only nine tables and a maximum capacity of 30.

Ash St. Cellar (bottom)
330 George Street, CBD
Tel: 02 9240 3000
www.merivale.com
Open: 10am–late Mon–Sat

Spilling out onto a paved, pedestrian laneway, the tiny Ash St. Cellar is a little slice of Paris in the heart of Sydney's business district, with an equally impressive wine list to boot. You may have to wait patiently for a seat outside, as the cluster of Champs-Élysées-style chairs and marble-topped tables can get quite busy, especially on the weekend. With snacky *spuntini* (Italian tapas) plates designed for sharing, it's a classy option for a mid-week tipple, with tables filled with an inner-city crowd and the inevitable dose of self-entitled suits. On weekends many punters bound for the playboy mansion wonderland of Ivy (down the lane in the same building) meet early for a swift drink and shared nibbles, though the chilled atmosphere and swift service encourages lingering. Monday nights (usually during summer months) are film nights – pay AU$35 for a film, wine and *spuntini*.

Bambini Wine Room (right)
185 Elizabeth Street, CBD
Tel: 02 9283 7098
www.bambinitrust.com.au
Open: 7am (5.30pm Sat)–late.
Closed Sundays.

With the headquarters of ACP magazines located just around the corner, Bambini Wine Room and its adjacent restaurant is a well-known haunt of glossy magazine editors and media execs, for work breakfasts, speedy afternoon macchiatos, business lunches and then lingering evenings spent sipping stellar drops from a Euro-centric wine list. The interiors are reminiscent of an elegant Parisian bar – every bit as glamorous as its clientele, with dark

hardwood furniture, Italian marble, Zoffany wallpaper, showpiece chandelier and sultry lounge music. For intimate tête-à-têtes, it's best to sit indoors, however, the best people-watching posts are outside, where the select number of tables on the footpath facing Hyde Park are the place to be seen for booze-fuelled power lunches, or an early evening glass of pinot. Wear your gladrags and darkest sunglasses.

Beach Haus *(left)*
5 Rosyln Street, Potts Point
Tel: 02 8065 1812
www.beachhaus.com.au
Open: 6pm–4am Wed–Sun

Tucked around a corner off the main drag at Kings Cross, Beach Haus is nowhere near the coast, but there's a definitive beach theme going on – the barstaff is kitted out in Le Coq Sportif sailor outfits, and the Hamptons-inspired décor features blond wood walls with a colossal mural of bikini-clad models cavorting on a beach. Don't wander in expecting a lot of room to swing – it's a teensy space with a teensy-weensy balcony – though there's a DJ toward the back of the room and people do start shimmying as the night develops. As far as drinks go, the emphasis is on cocktails and feeling special. You can order a shared cocktail served in vessels shaped like seashells, and take turns to sip it à la Lady and the Tramp through hand-crafted, platinum straws. If you've more cash to play with, phone ahead and reserve the butler chest – a Waterford chest/bar that will be set up privately for you and your entourage with a selection of

tipples, mixers, ice and even a personal butler to boss around for the evening.

Bungalow 8   *(right)*
8 The Promenade,
King Street Wharf, CBD
Tel: 02 9299 4660
www.bungalow8sydney.com
Open: daily, noon–1am (3am Thurs–Sat)

With a waterfront view over Darling Harbour, outdoor tables abuzz with a young, down-to-earth crowd and a striking modern design by Australian architect Dale Jones-Evans, Bungalow 8 toes the line between pub and bar – the sort of spot that morphs from a casual seafood 'n' drinks bistro by day into a cracking Sydney nightspot post-sunset, especially because slick cocktail bar The Loft is just upstairs. The interiors are inspiring, with hanging lamps of reed, illuminated bamboo and a DJ manning the decks on weekends, though the outdoor tables or booths are the money spots with views over the harbour. As far as tipples go, there's plenty to choose from and it's all decently-priced, with around 40 varieties of vodka and plenty of draught beers, including the award-winning Matilda Bay, 'Barking Duck' farmhouse ale. It's also a top choice for an informal lunch, especially on Tuesdays, when the city crowd converges for all-you-can-eat mussel feasts, served in traditional Belgian kilo pots with chunky fries and crusty bread.

Blu Bar   *(left)*
36th floor, Shangri-La Hotel,
176 Cumberland Street, The Rocks
Tel: 02 9250 6000.
Open: daily, 5pm (noon Fri)–1am;
(2am Fri/Sat, midnight Sun)

A 'Lost in Translation'-style hotel bar, Blu Bar sits on its lofty 36th floor throne with a seriously impressive view over Sydney Harbour. But the view is useless unless you've managed to wrangle a seat – while there are floor-to-ceiling windows, there are only a few window-facing barstools and high tables. Don't come here expecting a Saturday night atmosphere – Blu Bar is hotel bar and it feels like one, which isn't necessarily a shortcoming. With a requisite sophisticated door host and sultry lounge music, it has a classy ambience and the bar is manned by fine mixologists, who can craft a sublime array of (expensive) cocktails from your standard Martini right up to a AU$10,000 'Martini On The Rock', served with a diamond. For the less moneyed, slurp down a Wibble, a tangy mix of Plymouth Gin, Plymouth Sloe Gin, grapefruit and lemon juice, with a blackberry liqueur finish – it doesn't need a sparkler to impress. Come here for a pre-dinner

cocktail in time for the sunset – it will blow your socks off.

***

Café Pacifico   *(right)*
95 Riley Street, Darlinghurst
Tel: 02 9360 3811
www.cafepacifico.com.au
Open: 6pm–late Tues–Sat

A favourite haunt for tequila aficionados, this cantina-style bar and eatery deserves a boozer's trophy for its decadent array of 80 premium and rare tequilas that grace the shelves – it's easily the biggest range in Australia. The top drop is Partida Elegante Extra Añejo tequila, which, at AU$65 a shot, doesn't come cheap. At Pacifico, the service is straight-up, and all the tequila loving means there's a relaxed, friendly vibe. It's particularly decent for a hair-of-the-dog feast, washing away the damage with tasty *enchiladas*, *burritos* and other south-of-the-border staples, while sampling the impressive range of Mexican and South American beers, such as Dos Equis, Bohemia, Tecate and Quilmas. Pacifico's jugs of margaritas are potent and somewhat legendary – if you slosh through a few of these, don't be surprised if you end up busting out

drink...

some salsa moves on the bar, fiesta-style. ¡Olé!

The Commons *(left)*
Local Eating House & Bar

32 Burton Street, Darlinghurst
Tel: 02 9358 1487
www.thecommons.com.au
Open: daily, noon–midnight (1am Fri/Sat, 11.30pm Sun)

The Commons might only be a year old, but it already feels like a favourite pair of jeans. Set in a heritage terrace with original hand-cut sandstone walls and recycled hardwood floors, the communal dining tables encourage socialising, as does the plant-filled courtyard. It's the sort of place where you could easily pull up a wooden crate and strike up a conversation with a stranger and nobody would flinch. Already making a name for itself with hearty, organic produce sourced from regional farms, The Commons has also built up a fanbase for chilled-out boozing. Down a longneck in the courtyard during warmer weather, and head down to the basement cellar in winter – a perfect spot to nurse a tumbler of malt whiskey in a squishy leather armchair in front of an original fireplace. There's even a library down there – either thumb through some well-worn classics while you drink, or sign-up to borrow one for later. Burton Street itself is a little hub of cool, with numerous other bars (Pocket, Doctor Pong and 13B) all just across the road.

Eau de Vie *(right)*
Kirketon Hotel, 229 Darlinghurst Road, Darlinghurst
Tel: 02 9357 2470   www.eaudevie.com.au
Open: daily, 6pm–1am

This hidden gem of a bar in the back of the Kirketon Hotel is one of Sydney's classiest joints, designed to emulate a 1920s speakeasy and inspired by the owner's love of vintage cocktail paraphernalia. Keep an eye out for collectables like delicate French water fountains, Bohemian crystal decanters and even a 1930s cocktail shaker shaped like a lady's leg. This is not a party venue – more a refined drinking den with classy surrounds and even classier tunes, particularly on Thursdays when there's live jazz. It's a place where regulars return time and time again, dipping into their personal stash of booze kept under lock and key in personal lockers. There are more than 500 different types of spirits, a selection of boutique beers and craft wines, and some serious bartending at play here; cocktail aficionados will want to let Eau de Vie's suspender-clad bartenders mix up a kick-arse creation. They're easily some of Sydney's finest. If you're peckish, the bar offers a tasting menu with cheese- and mezze-style snacks.

Fico *(bottom)*
544 Bourke Street (enter via Nobbs Street), Surry Hills
Tel: 02 9699 2133
www.ficowinebar.com.au
Open: daily, 6–10pm

The discreet entrance, sexy jazz tunes and flickering red candles should give

drink...

137

you an idea that Fico isn't a rowdy drinking den. It's a place to woo a special someone, toasting one another with a fabulous glass of red in one of the bar's intimate nooks. The focus here is on wine and the staff is approachable, with knowledgeable sommeliers able to recommend from a carefully-crafted selection of 36 Australian and Italian wines. Most are sold by the glass, and each pack a punch when paired with Fico's thoughtful bar menu. Try the *salsiccette romane grigliate* (grilled pork and fennel sausages) with a savoury *nero d'avola*, for example. Snacky plates of antipasti like proscuitto, grissini and tender baby calamari rings should sate a grumbling tum, while penny-pinchers should get there between 6–7pm when Fico serves *aperitivo* (just like in Italy), allowing you to nibble at complimentary antipasti with every glass of wine. *Bellisimo!*

 Flinders Hotel *(top)*
65 Flinders Street, Darlinghurst
Tel: 02 9356 3622
www.theflindershotel.com.au
Open: 5pm–3am (5am Fri / Sat, midnight Sun). Closed Mondays.

Sydney's favourite dive bar, Flinders, was a decrepit old pub bought and renovated by restaurateur/club-owner Nick Mathers, Ksubi fashion label co-owner Paul Wilson and the city's Bang Gang DJs Gus Da Hoodrat and Jaime Doom. Not a great deal has been done to the interiors, with bent signs, stacks of beer cans and a wooden bar carved with graffiti sprayed everywhere. It's modelled on a classic American dive bar, so the drinks are hard and fast. Cocktails are a joy, however, and there's

no leaving until you've necked at least one Pickle Back, a shot of Jameson followed by a shot of pickle juice – so nasty it's good. Despite the dive bar tag, Flinders attracts a well-heeled, Eastern Suburbs crowd that likes to party hard, and the bar (rather dangerously) stays open until around 5am on rollicking weekends. Wednesday nights are devoted to hip-hop with weekends dominated by electro/indie/house tunes and podcasts. For food, there's plenty of bar snacks and scratchings downstairs and British colonial eats can be had upstairs at Duke Bistro (see Eat), a fab little joint presided over by chefs Thomas Lim (ex-Tetsuya's) and Mitch Orr.

 Gazebo Wine Garden *(bottom)*
2 Elizabeth Bay Road,
Elizabeth Bay
Tel: 02 9357 5333
www.thegazebos.com.au
Open: daily, 3pm (noon Thurs–Sun)– midnight

Gazebo is a favourite among the Sydney socialite set, with a refreshingly fun, frivolous attitude to wine. Though there's a temperature-controlled enomatic wine system and the place is staffed by some of Sydney's finest sommeliers, the menu itself is tongue-in-cheek, categorised by 'pink bits', 'unpronounceable' or 'slurpables'. With hanging ferns and vines, the Gazebo scene is bohemian garden party meets *Alice in Wonderland*, with semi-al fresco tables spilling out onto the streetside terrace, where you can get stuck into classic and house cocktails like the summertime favourites: jugs of Pimm's and sangria. The food isn't anything to write home about, but it's reasonably

drink...

139

good value and with a garden party atmosphere that will win you over; it's never stale, with regular art exhibitions and events like wine- or cheese-tasting.

■ The Glenmore *(left)*
Rooftop Hotel
96 Cumberland Street, The Rocks
Tel: 02 9247 4794
www.glenmorerooftophotel.com.au
Open: daily, 10am–midnight (1am Sat/Sun)

If it's a sparkling Sydney day and you want to drink a frosted schooner in the sun on a rooftop, this is the place. The Glenmore is one of a few pubs left in the historic area of The Rocks which dates back to pre-World War II. It might look like a typical Aussie pub downstairs, with tables spilling out on the pavement, interiors decked out with scungy carpet and wood panelling aplenty, but the real draw of this place is its rooftop beer garden – it has views over the harbour to the Opera House and beyond. Super-relaxed and super-friendly, head up here in summer for barbecues and 'Big Jug Sundays', where you can pitch up with a jug of sangria or Pimm's, order from a pub menu that features burgers, schnitzel, salads and bar snacks (all under AU$20), and top up your tan. Get here early if it's a day of national importance, like Australia Day or a public holiday – the place gets rammed.

■ Grasshopper *(right)*
Temperance Lane (between RM Williams & Oakley on George St), CBD
Tel: 02 9947 9025

www.thegrasshopper.com.au
Open: noon–1am. Closed Sundays.

Where do we start with a bar this magnificent? Grasshopper is a miniscule drinkery tucked away in a grungy, urban city lane. It's so hidden away that finding it almost requires GPS, though invariably on any given night the place will be packed with a mix of laid-back city workers and hipsters. There's not a smidgen of attitude in the petite basement space, decked out in casual-chic style with squishy ottomans, low tables and kung-fu posters. You'll need to do some elbow jostling if you want to prop up the bar, which only has a few barstools. Most drinkers tend to spill out into the laneway with their cocktails (numbered one to 10 and served in jam jars), pulling up old milk crates to sit on, and giving the place an illegal street party vibe. If you're early, it's worth checking out the small upstairs dining area where Grasshopper's restaurant serves up a simple, classic bistro menu. Some of the snacks are also available downstairs – try the moreishly tasty homemade duck parfait and organic bread. Delish.

■ Hemmesphere *(top)*
Level 4, 252 George Street, CBD
Tel: 02 9240 3000
www.merivale.com
Open: 5.30pm–midnight (3am Thurs–Sat). Closed Sundays.

Easily one of Sydney's classiest cocktail bars, Hemmesphere is a stalwart of the Sydney scene and one for the discerning cocktail lover. It's accessed via an elevator from the ground floor

of the Establishment hotel and when the doors open you'll be greeted by a jawdroppingly stunning host and led through a sprawling Ottoman era-style room, with trapeze artist-high ceilings, soft seating, dim lighting and a DJ spinning sultry lounge. Hemmesphere is a bar for those with refined tastes and this is reflected in the menu – it's exquisite, with hand-cut ice, premium malt whiskies, cognac, brandy cigars and vintage Champagne. Nibbles come in the form of a delicate Japanese menu from the adjacent Sushi e restaurant (see Eat). All in all, you'd be hard pressed to find a better venue in which to ply your object of passion with exotic cocktails. Expect to part with a bit more bread than you would elsewhere, but it's worth it.

....

Hunky Dory Social Club *(left)*

215 Oxford St, Darlinghurst
Tel: 02 9331 0442
www.hdsc.com.au
Open: daily, 11am–late

Filled with a frat-tastic blend of young models, femi-men, porkpie hats, tatts and eyebrow piercings, Hunky Dory is one of the newest rooftop bars to launch within the past year and the crowd is super-cool, Sydney-style. There's lots of exposed brick, heavy wood and the décor is edgy; think a couple of worn Chesterfields, chandeliers from a French mansion in Morocco and bar menus laid out in vintage Golden Books – remember those? The main bar and DJ are on the first floor, reached by walking up a flight of stairs next to Bruno's Italian Cuisine. Best order cocktails from here – the upstairs bar doesn't stock as decent a range of tipple, but the space opens out to a seriously cool, Manhattan-esque rooftop area. If you can bag yourself a seat up here, you've done well. Basking in the glow of a neon-lit billboard above and littered with a chaotic jumble of pot plants, this appealing spot is simply made for al fresco drinking – go for an ice-cold longneck beer, served, somewhat ironically, in a brown paper bag.

....

Ivy Lounge *(middle)*
330 George Street, CBD
Tel: 02 9243 3000
www.merivale.com
Open: 11am (6pm Sat)–late.
Closed Sundays.

Take a fat wallet and put on your party hat, because this multi-level ode to drinking, dining and carousing is one of the city's most debauched evening playgrounds. Sydney's resident bar baron Justin Hemmes has spent around AU$150-million on this galactic-sized playpen, which has numerous bars, cocktail lounges, a Sailors Thai restaurant and hundreds of staff, including three full-time gardeners and a full-time florist. The interior is like stepping into the sort of bar a stylish Willy Wonka may have conjured up, with astro turf, white marble, ferns growing wildly and a huge Japanese maple that spans between two levels. The main bar and Lawn Bar are for the wild and care-free, but more discerning drinkers should make a beeline to The Den and The Lounge. With their Chesterfield sofas, velvet drapes, both are styled in

an elegant Art Deco fashion and cater to cocktail aficionados with top-shelf tipples, cigars and mannerly staff. With so many venues to manage and so many eager party-goers to please, Ivy's doormen are notoriously tough with their velvet ropes, and while it's true the poseur ratio can be remarkably high at times, an evening spent here is good, clean, riotous fun.

Ivy Pool Club *(right)*
Level 4, 330 George Street, CBD
Tel: 02 9243 3000
www.merivale.com
Open: noon (5pm Sat)–late. Closed Sundays & Mondays.

Entrance to this South Beach Miami meets Palm Springs wonderland is carefully restricted and as the name suggests, its centrepiece is the outdoor pool; the playground for Sydney's genetically blessed. It can be virtually empty on cold winter nights, but in the summer there's nowhere in the city quite like it; especially when the Champagne flows and bikini-clad women

cavort to Sydney's top DJs. Make sure to look out for the infamous old man grooving around the pool area. You'll know exactly who we're talking about. The downsides? There's bound to be a fair few pleased with themselves bankers hanging around, and the menu is far pricier than most Sydney bars, with a range of cocktails, spirits, local and imported beer, extensive global wine list, and rather surprisingly, pretty darn good pizza. The private cabanas that overlook the pool are usually reserved for members and the minted few, but can be reserved ahead of time by persuasive laymen. Laymen, however, are unlikely to be invited up to the Ivy Penthouse on level six, a (mostly) exclusive member's bar with a fur-draped, sunken circular lounge, poker room, balcony and hot tub with views over the Pool Club. If you're attempting to

access either, just be sure to dust off something half-decent to wear as the door policy tends to weed out undesirables (and the fashion-unconscious).

Lo-Fi (left)
First Floor, 383 Bourke Street, Darlinghurst
Tel: 02 9311 3100
www.wearelofi.com.au
Open: 5pm–3am Thurs–Sun

Lo-Fi was one of the first bars to jump on Sydney's current design obsession – the deconstructed-on-purpose look, which translates to ripped-out ceilings, exposed air ducts and the hiring of local street artists, who adorn the walls with rotating graffiti murals. It's all stylishly executed – check out the kitsch lamps covered with old Mega-

drink...

deth and Nirvana albums when you order a drink – then make for the al fresco balcony. Commanding a great view over Taylor Square below, it's covered with astro turf and vintage vinyl furniture. With an art gallery upstairs, Lo-fi is so on-the-pulse cool, the place literally heaves come the weekend – expect to rub shoulders with grown-up emos and cashed-up advertising and PR execs. Drinks-wise, there are classic cocktails aplenty like negronis, dark 'n' stormies and Pisco sours, but our money is on a frosty beer served in a longneck, preferably on the balcony at dusk. Booya!

The Loft _(right)_
3 Lime Street, King Street Wharf
Tel: 02 9299 4770
www.theloftsydney.com

Open: daily, 4pm (noon Thurs–Sat)–1am (3am Thurs–Sat)

Overlooking King Street Wharf with 240-degree harbour views from its decked balcony, The Loft is a sophisticated watering hole. A few years ago it was considered queen bee among Sydney socialites, and though a slew of other bar openings has meant that the fickle have moved on, it still remains a chic spot for an expertly-mixed sunset cocktail. There are more than 26 on offer – try the Kaffir Southsider made with Plymouth gin, lime, Kaffir lime leaves, mint and sugar. The Loft's interiors are all class, with toffee-coloured leather banquettes, plush carpets, filigree wooden panels and private lounge areas with table service. Though mostly sedate, the atmosphere perks up late at night and during the weekend, when

DJs spin lounge and funk that pulls in some of the crowd from Bungalow 8 downstairs. Due to the size of both the bars, and the fact they're located in the same block, the King Street Wharf area always seems abuzz with a diverse inner-city crowd – especially on a sparkling Sydney day.

 The London *(left*
234 Darling Street, Balmain
Tel: 02 9555 1377
www.londonhotel.com.au
Open: daily, 11am–midnight Mon–Sat;
noon–10pm Sun

An institution in Sydney, The London Hotel has been around since 1870 and it's a cherished local pub for Balmain residents – countless schooners and belly laughs have been had while perched on its famous balcony, which has a long wooden bench and bar stools that overlook trendy Darling Street below. The vibe is incredibly casual – this is a quintessential Aussie local made for casual beers and ciders, and hearty plates of better-than-average pub grub – think piri-piri chicken, avocado and grilled haloumi salad, burgers and beer-battered fish and chips. You can even bash out a few lazy games of pool in the upstairs bar. If there's no room on the ever-popular balcony, the main Jarrah-panelled drinking area is just as appealing – it's flanked by a centre square bar, crafted at perfect elbow-leaning height.

The Lord Dudley *(right)*
236 Jersey Road, Woollahra
Tel: 02 9327 5399

www.lorddudley.com.au
Open: daily, 11am (noon Sun)–11pm
(midnight Thurs–Sat 11am, 10pm Sun)

Brits missing their traditional London pubs will feel right at home at the Lord Dudley, a well-loved corner drinkery in the leafy, well-to-do suburb of Woollahra – Sydney's version of Primrose Hill. Owned by affable publican James Couche, it's one of the Eastern Suburbs' best-known pubs, with a shock of foliage spiralling over the entrance and drinkers converging for beers and chats outside on the footpath. With its wood panelling, English paraphernalia, antiques and old-stone fireplace, the ground floor bar is as welcoming and comfortable as any in rural England, with a bounty of beer, cider and ale on tap. There's also a dart room, upstairs levels that open during the evening and a restaurant that serves quintessential pub grub – think pork pies, pickled eggs and bangers and mash. It's also only a stroll away from Paddington Bowling Club, where you can have a wobbly game of barefoot lawn bowls in the sun. What's not to love?

 Love Tilly Devine *(bottom)*
91 Crown Lane, Darlinghurst
Tel: 02 9326 9297
www.lovetillydevine.com
Open: 4pm–midnight Tues–Sat

The newest, cosiest and most congenial 'small' bar to launch in the Eastern Suburbs is a splendid little wine joint named after an infamous bordello madame who lorded it up in the 1920s and 30s around Sydney. It's a marvellously welcoming spot, with tables and chairs

The Lord Dudley HOTEL

crowded together downstairs, a minuscule upstairs bit with banquettes and tables, and the sound of vinyl records playing over the bustle of the open kitchen, which pumps out tasty plates like bruschetta and slow-cooked octopus. The owners are religious about their wine and the list is comprehensive, with at least 300 wines from all corners of the world on offer. The sommeliers can help make sense of it all, whether you want to quaff a Grenache Blend from Southern Rhône or share a South Australian field blend served in a classic glass pint bottle for AU$25. Some of the tables might be clustered a little too close together for comfort, but what's a bit of elbow knocking when you're halfway through a cracking Muscadet?

Madame Fling Flong (left)
169 King Street, Newtown
Tel: 02 9565 2471
www.madameflingflong.com.au
Open: daily, 4pm (3pm Thurs–Sun)–
11pm (midnight Thurs–Sat, 10pm Sun)

A retro, bohemian wonderland, Madame Fling Flong is unashamedly one of Sydney's kookiest, most kitsch bars, where gaudy pink walls and mismatched vintage furniture assault the eyes and a potent cocktail list assaults the tastebuds. It's very 'Newtown' – a stroll along King Street below should give you a hint as to what that means; packed with cheap Thai restaurants, thrift stores and pubs, the area attracts university students, performance artists and the alternative. It's a hugely popular spot for a casual mid-week drink, especially on the legendary

Tuesday night movie nights. Madame Fling Flong favours cult flicks and the price (AU$20) includes a glass of wine or beer and mezze from Soni's Tapas (same owners), which serves up a decent tapas menu should all the kookiness have worked up an appetite.

Mille Vini (right)
397 Crown Street, Surry Hills
Tel: 02 9357 3366
Open: daily, 5–11pm (midnight
Thurs–Sat, 10pm Sun)

This oh-so hip Surry Hills wine joint is usually always abuzz – a good choice if you've been wandering the length of the hipster-happy Crown Street searching for an intimate spot for a glass of wine. The name should give you a hint that Mille Vini is an ode to the good stuff, with floor-to-ceiling walls of bottles, tasteful sandstone walls, exposed wooden beams and a mix of Surry Hills locals nattering away while snacking on *spuntini*-style Italian bites. There will be something to suit even the most finicky wine-lover, with more than 300 wines on the menu from Australia, New Zealand and Europe, many available by the glass. If *spuntini* doesn't fill the hunger gap, there are plenty of restaurants along buzzing Crown Street that will.

Opera Bar (top)
Lower Concourse Level,
Sydney Opera House
Tel: 02 9247 1666
www.operabar.com.au
Open: daily, 11.30am–late

Sprawled directly on the harbour front on the lower Opera House concourse, this open-air bar never fails to stop wide-eyed tourists in their tracks. It's been described 'the best beer garden in the world', which isn't an exaggeration. With the water mere inches away and spectacular views across the harbour, it's the sort of place Sydneysiders take international guests for sundowners, and end up staying on well into the night. The length of the bar is undercover, however, the majority of the terrace area has little more than a few umbrellas for shelter, leaving it at mercy to the elements. This means on a balmy summer afternoon it can be (as Aussies would say) a 'shitfight' to snare a seat, while on a rainy night it's a ghost town. If you've lucked out with a glorious Sydney day, there are few better spots to be, sipping on a chilled glass of wine, draught beer or cocktail in-hand and gawping at the megawatt view while a jazz band plays. Best of all, you don't have to dress up – t-shirts and flip-flops are uniform.

Piano Room   *(left)*
1 Bayswater Road, Kings Cross
Tel: 02 9357 5522
www.trademarkhotel.com.au
Open: 7pm (8pm Fri / Sat)–late Weds–Sat

Basked in the red neon glow of the iconic Coca-Cola sign, the Piano Room is in the heart of Sydney's red light district with a lofty vista over William Street. It's a classy live music venue with a grand piano and the invariable nightly rota of jazz trios or solo saxophonists and DJs. As you'd expect, it's an elegant, genteel spot; a good 'un to canoodle with a foxy date for a pre- or post-meal cocktail, though you could easily sink into one of the plush Chesterfield sofas and spend all night feeding each other tapas treats, like fresh figs with goat's cheese and prosciutto or seared scallops with avocado and vanilla oil. Best to phone ahead and reserve yourself a nook – the doormen can be particularly picky. You can

hardly blame them, given the notorious hoo-haa of Kings Cross.

Pocket *(middle)*
13 Burton Street, Darlinghurst
Tel: 02 9380 7002
ww.pocketsydney.com.au
Open: daily, 10am (5pm Mon)–midnight

This gritty, hip, semi-underground space attracts the crème of Sydney's hipster crowd, with more non-prescription glasses and stovepipe jeans than you can poke a swizzle stick at. The design is edgy and on-the-pulse urban, with stencil-art graffiti and murals by respected local street artists adorning the walls, mis-matched armchairs, Chesterfield sofas, and a jumble of curios stashed in every spare space – think vintage train tickets, National Geographic mags and urban trainers. The barmen take their jobs seriously here, so order with confidence - the focus is on superlative, expertly-made cocktail classics like negronis, brambles or 'pimped' classics. Wines are available by the carafe and if you're peckish, Pocket serves both sweet and savoury crepes.

Rockpool Bar & Grill *(right)*
66 Hunter Street, CBD
Tel: 02 8078 1900
www.rockpool.com.au
Open: noon (5.30pm Sat)–midnight.
Closed Sundays.

With an awards list as long as the cocktail menu, Rockpool Bar & Grill is unequivocally one of Sydney's best bars. Set adjacent to chef Neil Perry's decadent city restaurant (see Eat) the design is as much of a delight as the bar itself; think original Art Deco interiors, hardwood and leather furniture and towering green marble columns. Mixing drinks beneath an eye-popping Riedel glass feature – there are 2,682 glasses, in case you were wondering –

are some of Sydney's finest bartenders who serve superior top-shelf tipples. The bar's premium rare spirits and wines are sourced from auction houses or wine merchants, the tonic water is made in-house and beer includes a AU$24 bottle of Chimay Blanche, made by Trappist monks in Belgium. The cocktail menu covers all tastes and whims, but it would be silly not to order a cocktail from the stellar range of American classics like the Side Car or the Mai Tai. It's also a time-honoured Sydney tradition to prop up the bar for the evening with a pinot and Perry's famous full-blood Wagyu burger. In a word, unforgettable.

 The Rum Diaries *(top)*
288 Bondi Road, Bondi
Tel: 02 9300 0440
www.therumdiaries.com.au
Open: daily, 6pm–late

A pilgrimage to this laid-back Bondi drinking and tapas den is like Haj for the rum aficionado; there are more than 80 types of the good stuff on offer here from across the globe, and the bar's Holy Grail is Havana Club Maximo at a cool AU$150 per serve. Catering to a mostly effortlessly hip Bondi crowd, bowler-hatted barmen mix up Cuba libres, mai tais and more Hemingway daiquiris than even its namesake boozehound could have quaffed. Even if rum doesn't rock your boat, there's something hugely appealing about this friendly bar probably due to the cheery staff, who do their best to make you feel at home. Interiors are casual, hip and ambient with lots of warm, recycled wood and curios like chandeliers and an old piano (which works – in case you want to have a bash). The food isn't half bad, either – pitch up at one of the tables and select tapasy bites from paddock and sea, or from the well-priced 'menus for two' section.

Shady Pines Saloon *(bottom)*
Shop 4, 256 Crown Street
(enter via laneway), Darlinghurst
www.shadypinessaloon.com
Open: daily, 4pm–midnight

The ultimate gritty dive bar, owners Anton Forte and Jason Scott originally wanted to call this basement bar The Swillhouse but the conservatives at Sydney City Council weren't impressed. It didn't matter in the end, because they settled on naming the bar Shady Pines Saloon and the place has become a favourite haunt for trendy twenty- and thirty-something fashion denizens. The theme is bull buckin' wild west, with bowls of unshelled peanuts, wooden barrels, carved Indian chief statues and 'wanted dead or alive' posters. The affable twang of country and western music plays in the background while punters slouch over the long wooden bar – the only thing missing is swinging saloon doors. This isn't the place to order a low-carb beer or a pre-mixed bottle – barmen serve up hard liquor, with kick-arse mint juleps and whisky sours, premium spirits like High West American whisky, and tinnies and craft beers like Sierra Nevada Pale Ale. Giddy up!

Small Bar *(left)*
48 Erskine Street , CBD
Tel: 02 9279 0782
www.smallbar.net.au
Open: 10.30am (5.30pm Sat)–midnight.
Closed Sundays.

Forever famous as the first 'small' bar of Sydney's small bar revolution, this cosy city bar isn't as pint-sized as you'd think. Spread over three levels in a quirky city terrace, the rear of the bar overlooks a paved pedestrian laneway with both a downstairs bar and a bar on the main level. It feels more like a university frathouse than a bar, and there's always enough space to nab a cosy armchair or squashy lounge to sit on with a mate or two (no more) and a glass of plonk. Wander up the narrow wooden staircases to the upper levels to net one of the coveted stools on the balconies that overlooks Sussex Lane, or head out to the laneway if the weather's fine. As one of the few character bars near Sydney's business district, the place is most lively during the post-working day drink rush, where 'tude-free city workers converge to swig artisanal beer like Beez Neez or Mountain Goat Steam Ale. There's a great little selection of wines, too, and plates to share like antipasto, skewers and ploughman's lunch. Call ahead to reserve one of the laneway tables.

Sticky *(right)*
182 Campbell Street (enter via Taggarts Lane), Darlinghurst
www.tablefor20.blogspot.com
Open: 6.30pm–midnight Wed–Sat

Clandestine, cool and a favourite haunt of in-the-know industry types, Sticky is one of Sydney's most covert bars above one of Sydney's most covert eateries, Table For 20 – also owned by Michael Fantuz (see Eat). To gain entry you have to walk down a deserted laneway, press a door buzzer and cross your fingers. Once upstairs, the interiors are dark and moody, with candelabra chandeliers, heavy red curtains and plush armchairs where it's all too easy to spend the entire night quaffing a cracking red from Sticky's impressive wine list. The bartenders are an impressive bunch, too, ready and willing to mix up thoughtful cocktails with panache – choose from their suggestions chalked up on the blackboard behind the bar. The beauty of Sticky is that even though it's been around for a year or so, it continues to fly well under the radar of the average bargoer – meaning it's never too busy and never filled with undesirables.

Time to Vino *(bottom)*
Lower Level, Diamant Hotel,
2-14 Kings Cross Road, Potts Point
Tel: 02 9380 4252
www.timetovino.com
Open: daily, 5–10.30pm (midnight Fri/Sat)

Clint Hillery is one of Australia's finest sommeliers with awards and accolades aplenty, and this wine bar-slash-restaurant at the foot of the Diamant Hotel is a labour of his love. The business began as a small bar in Sydney's Little Italy Quarter, while the new locale has much more elbow room and the same intimacy. It's the perfect spot

to sneak away to and sniff, slosh and quaff through a truly smashing list of vino from around the world, especially on Sunday and Monday when carafes are at glass prices. There are more than 35 wines by the glass, 200 bottles and a vast array of half bottles, fortifieds, sherries et al. As for solids, the pairing of food and wine is an art form that Time to Vino likes to call 'booze food', with a share menu to pick at titled 'Waiting for Friends', some sit-down options and some noteworthy options for solo drinkers, who are welcomed with open arms. An unpretentious spot to spend a few – or many – memorable hours cradling a wine glass.

 Tokonoma Shochu *(top)*
Bar & Lounge
490 Crown Street, Surry Hills
Tel: 02 9357 6100
www.toko.com.au
Open: daily, 5.30pm–midnight

As any seasoned tippler will tell you, rum, gin and vodka are so last year. Shochu is where it's at, and Tokonoma, with its exhaustive list of sake and shochu, is the place to get it. Along with serving sublime Japanese cuisine, this stylish, street-level bar takes a leaf out of the Nobu or Zuma book with loungey leather nooks, easy-on-the-eye wood panelling, sexy lounge tunes played by the resident DJ and decadent cocktails. They're mostly fresh, zingy Japanese-inspired more-ish creations like the Sashimitini, which blends gin, Hakutake Shiro shochu and ginger, and comes garnished with a slice of wasabi-dipped salmon. If you're prone to excess (who isn't?)

your liver will love you for guzzling down one of Tokonoma's specially created 'health' tonics, which are made by macerating 'superfruits' like papaya, goji and barley fruits in shochu. As for the crowd, Tokonoma has netted itself some prime real estate on Sydney's hipster-mile Crown Street, luring in the on-the-pulse style mavens and media types.

 Victoria Room *(bottom)*
Level 1, 235 Victoria Street,
Darlinghurst
Tel: 02 9357 4488
www.thevictoriaroom.com
Open: 6pm (noon Sat, 1pm Sun)–
midnight (2am Fri). Closed Mondays.

With potted palm trees, wooden screens, gilded, regal armchairs and classic British Raj décor, Victoria Room was one of the first Sydney bars to jump on the high-tea train, serving afternoon cucumber sandwiches and pots of Darjeeling at weekends to groups of tittering females. At night, this sultry bar adjusts its hat to ply punters with stiff drinks from a brilliant cocktail menu – try Charlie's Caribbean Tipple (aged Appleton rum with Drambuie, almond syrup and orange bitters), or if you're in a group, the Victoria Room Punch Bowl serves four. The bar's colonial atmosphere and moody lighting lends itself to intimate evening chinwagging with friends – either by the bar or in one of the more intimate crannies of chaise lounges and regal armchairs. There's entertainment in the form of DJs or a live muso tinkling the ivories of the piano, especially during the Sunday evening

drink...

Performance Carnival, a bohemian hoot of roving mime artists, burlesque beauties, sultry tango dancers and even acrobats. At the time of writing, owners were discussing installing a trapeze swing high up in the rafters.

The Welcome Hotel (right)
91 Evans Street, Rozelle
Tel: 02 9810 1323
www.thewelcomehotel.com
Open: daily, 11am–10pm (midnight Fri/Sat)

As locals would say, you're always welcome at 'The Welly'. This classic Inner West pub is one of the area's most friendly and atmospheric watering holes, in typical Aussie-Irish style, with a leafy heated courtyard with chunky benches and ferns scattered about, a traditional wood-panelled bar and an excellent pub menu. Don't be fooled by the casualness, though – the Welly's food is more contemporary bistro fare than pub grub, with soufflés, lamb, spatchcock and extremely well-priced steak. There's a range of local and imported beer, ale and cider on tap to suit all tastes, including Bulmers, Kilkenny and Old Speckled Hen, and entertainment in the form of classic rock bands and trivia nights. This is a great pub to head to if you're in the mood for casual boozing, with genuinely friendly pub service, free of pomp and ceremony.

Winery by Gazebo (bottom)
285a Crown Street, Surry Hills
Tel: 02 9331 0833
www. thegazebos.com.au
Open: daily, 3pm (noon Thurs–Sun)–midnight

When you first see Winery, you wouldn't be blamed for thinking someone went and raided the set of *Willy Wonka* and *Alice in Wonderland*, throwing in a tangle of stag heads, animal hide, hanging ferns and walls of bright green foliage for good measure. The design of this bar deserves some kind of a gong for its bold, brash and showy sense of style. The same can be said of the staff and the crowd, an eclectic, trendy bunch of Surry Hills locals and wine nerds. It doesn't take a brain of epic proportions to work out wine is the focus here, with more than 50 variations available. Like its sister venue Gazebo, Winery divides its plonk into tongue-in-cheek categories like 'slurpable' and 'unpronounceable', though don't be fooled – the place has some remarkable drops, including 1995 Grange, available by the glass for AU\$79. Unless you're really hungry, skip the average mains for sharing plates, and settle in for a frolicsome evening. There's plenty of space over the three split-levels, but the place to be during summer is the tables and chairs outside on the paved street level – jug of Pimm's at-the-ready! Sadly, the stiffs at Sydney City Council have regulated this space, meaning you will be herded indoors after 6pm to appease Winery's narky neighbours.

Wine Library (left)
18 Oxford Street, Woollahra
Tel: 02 9328 1600
Open: daily, 9am–10pm (6pm Sun)

Got a hankering for fantastic wine and Italian snacks? This slick hole-in-the-wall wine bar is a winner for casual drinks 'n' eats. It's located just at the top of Paddington's famous shopping strip (post-credit card splurge tipple, perhaps?) and the place is damn popular. There are only 48 seats, but every single one – whether it's at the eat-at bar, near the front windows, alongside the wall or in the tiny back courtyard – will be taken, that's almost a guarantee. The best seats, however, are at the zinc bar lined with stools. Owned by the operators of Buzo restaurant, the 10-year-old Italian stalwart just around the corner on Jersey Road, Wine Library's list is hefty and interesting, and the sharing plates are incredibly well-priced for the quality – think salami-heaped charcuterie boards, pate and cheeses, *bocadillos*, scotch eggs and more. It's Italian without being in-your-face Italian, though barstaff will grin ear-to-ear if you order a negroni. Get in early and enjoy.

 Zeta *(bottom)*
Hilton Hotel, 4/488 George Street, CBD
Tel: 02 9265 6070
www.zetabar.com.au
Open: 5pm–late. Closed Sundays.

A slinky seductress, Zeta is set inside the Hilton hotel, with a knockout terrace that overlooks George Street and the elaborate Romanesque dome of the Queen Victoria Building. The interiors conjure up a Moroccan harem, with alluring North Africa-inspired ottomans and lounges, exotic fabrics and sexy hostesses that seem to glide rather than walk. Not a fan of Morocco? Or Sydney, for that matter? Then let Zeta bartenders whisk you away to a Havana street bar, or perhaps a Hawaiian beach. Always a forerunner in the cocktail game, Zeta's

molecular mixologists have a knack of revamping the humble cocktail into a so-called 'sensory experience'. The Havana experience, for example, will have you sitting at the bar blindfolded, sipping a mojito and inhaling a cigar-scented mist while listening to salsa through an iPod. Want your mojito slightly more fantastico? Then go for the deconstructed version, cryogenically frozen with LN2 and served as a sorbet in a mini waffle cone. Or chomp on a deconstructed Martini jelly, finished with a puff of vermouth 'air'. Regular drinkers need not worry, though, Zeta doesn't only serve wizz-bang concoctions and bartenders are happy to oblige even if you just want a plain old G&T instead of popcorn-infused rum. Though it sounds kind of boring now, doesn't it?

Manly Wharf Hotel

drink...

snack...

Melbourne might be the most European of Australia's cities, but Sydneysiders are religious about coffee. Test it out – suggest meeting up at Starbucks to your Sydney friend, and watch the incredulous expression spread across their face. Be it cappuccino, soy latte, macchiato, piccolo or plain old flat white (coffee with milk), you would be hard pressed to find a decent Sydney café failing to serve expertly-brewed beans, made by baristas who view their craft with all the seriousness of a neurosurgeon. We've listed the best beaneries here, including cafés producing their own superlative blends with on-site roasteries, namely Allpress, Toby's Estate and Little Marionette.

Then there's breakfast. Be it a hole-in-the-wall joint in an edgier suburb like Surry Hills to bustling CBD coffee counters and pooch-friendly beachside hangouts, it's a time-honoured tradition to indulge in a long, leisurely breakfast, especially on Sunday mornings, when lingering over bacon and eggs with newspapers spread out on the table is seen as a ritual. Most cafés have breakfast whittled down to an art form, serving more organic eggs, bircher mueslis, artisanal breads and freshly-squeezed juices than you can poke a fork at. During summer, it would be a sorry loss to eat your eggs without a view of the ocean, a beach or a harbour at the very least, so head north to Bathers Pavilion, Burnt Orange, Barrenjoey House Palm Beach and Ripples for exceptional brekkies with a water view. The urban (but no less appealing) Café Giulia in Chippendale is always a winner if you're ducking through the inner-city. In Bondi, try the laid-back Gertrude & Alice, and for breakfast and a dip in the east, Nielsen Park Kiosk Café.

Australians might be relaxed, but Sydneysiders are busy people who need to refuel quickly without putting the words fast and food together, which means lots of good options for food on-the-go. During the day, there are plentiful spots to grab on-the-run sandwiches, wraps or toasties, huge salads or Wagyu burgers – try Plan B in

the city for a burger fix. Sushi train joints are a dime a dozen, though streetwise eateries like Miss Chu bring the chaos and pungent flavours of hawker Vietnamese to the pavement – the rice paper rolls really are top-notch. For sweet snacks, most cafés display typical treats like soft banana breads wrapped in cling-film and homemade muffins on their counter, but most up the ante and go to the source, buying their stock from Black Star in Newtown, which offers a cheeky, artisanal take on pastries – the humble gingerman here is known as ginger ninja. For delicate French pastries made in classical Parisian style, head to La Renaissance Patisserie in The Rocks – don't leave without sampling their famous macaron, sweet ganache encased in delicate, pastel-coloured meringue shells.

For an unfussy feed at night, there are numerous on-trend eateries serving casual meals in pomp-free settings, with no white linen tablecloths in sight, which suits the *laissez-faire* attitudes locals are famous for. Look out for the neighbourly Bronte Road Bistro and Bar H, which both have the option of dining at an eat-at bar, a god-send for solo diners who want to avoid the indignity of sitting at a table alone. To snack in the great outdoors, do as Sydneysiders do and hunt down a barbecued chicken shop, because eating a chook 'n' chips with tabouleh salad on a picnic rug or at the beach is as Australian as a kangaroo. Which Australians eat, too, coincidentally. We've listed the super-dooper Chargrill Charlies, where any Aussie actor or celeb worth their chicken salt goes. To top it off, you can't truly say you've been and done Sydney without a visit to Harry's Café de Wheels, which serves famous meat pies – so legendary, even Elton John, Frank Sinatra and Brooke Shields have eaten one.

About Life *(top)*
605 Darling Street, Rozelle
Tel: 02 8755 1333
www.aboutlife.com.au
Open: daily, 6am (7am Sat/Sun)–8pm (7pm Fri–Sun)

Simply walking into About Life is enough to make you feel healthy. The organic and health food supermarket is chock-full of wares with aisle after aisle of spirulina, hummus and organic groceries. If you just need a quick bite, grab a healthy pitta roll, salad or bottled organic juice from the takeaway fridge. Just near the entrance there's a constantly busy counter area that pumps out freshly-squeezed super juices and coffee, and around the side is a relaxed café, where Rozelle locals converge after the Saturday markets to flick through newspapers or the health magazines and drink Fairtrade coffee. It's all very laid-back and the food is healthy and delicious – think plump pumpkin and feta frittatas, wraps and salads, smoothies and bran muffins. Vegetarians, vegans and coeliacs will be in their element.

Allpress Roastery Café *(left)*
58 Epsom Road, Rosebery
Tel: 02 9662 8288
www.allpressespresso.com.au
Open: 7am–3pm Mon–Fri; 8am–2pm Sat

If you're visiting Sydney, the industrial area of Rosebery probably won't be on the itinerary. But Sydneysiders who are serious about their beans make the effort. The site functions primarily as a roastery set up by owner Michael Allpress and the attached café func-

tions as the self-described 'working billboard'. Come caffeine hour there are cars circling the block, while a steady stream of businessmen, arts students and mums with prams snake out the door. The business of roasting Arabica carries on out the back, while freshly-roasted blends and single origin coffees are swiftly poured out the front, along with a limited café menu – mostly Italian panini sandwiches. When it's busy, service can be a bit Soup Nazi, but true coffee-lovers will take it in their stride.

Bar Coluzzi *(right)*
322 Victoria Street, Darlinghurst
Tel: 02 9380 5420
Open: daily, 5am–7pm

Among the bursting-at-the-seams-with-eateries Victoria Street and right next door to Latteria (nothing like a bit of friendly café rivalry), Bar Coluzzi stands proud (and quite rightly so). It's the oldest café on the strip and was opened in 1957 by Italian-born Luigi Coluzzi, who was one of the middle-weight boxing greats of the 1950s and, some would say, the man who rescued Australia from the heinous clutches of instant coffee. The walls of this miniscule café are plastered with photos of Luigi pumping his fists ringside, though unfortunately the gregarious Italian sold the business in 2000 and opened up a new café in the suburb of Randwick. Nevertheless, Coluzzi's colourful regulars, powerbrokers and celebrities still call it home. Get a stool out on the pavement, except in the early morning, when the 50-strong

snack...

'Coluzzi bunch' (cyclists) descends on the café in their Lycra-clad droves.

....

Bar H *(left)*
80 Campbell Street, Surry Hills
Tel: 02 9280 1980
www.barhsurryhills.com
Open: noon–3pm Thurs/Fri, 6pm–late Mon–Sat

With wide windows that overlook the urban pavements, design-conscious locals and warehouse apartments of Surry Hills, Bar H is a slick yet casual neighbourhood eatery that isn't trying to be a restaurant, meaning it's perfect for a glass of Champagne and an eat-and-go light dinner, or a morning macchiato and toast. Forget about dull bar snacks, however – the food has some bonafide culinary cred; think liver pâté with shaved foie-gras, soft mulloway sashimi, Ortiz anchovies with lemon and fresh salads of flavourful heirloom tomatoes and chunks of ricotta. Dark and moody, with lots of low lighting, there are only a handful of tables but it's best to snare a spot at the eat-in bar and order a coffee or a drop from the attractive floor-to-ceiling feature-wall wine rack. Smart enough for a planned date, and casual enough for a spontaneous walk-in.

....

Barrenjoey House *(right)*
Palm Beach
1108 Barrenjoey Road, Palm Beach
Tel: 02 9974 4001
www.barrenjoeyhouse.com.au
Open: daily, 11.30am–9pm (10pm Fri/Sat)

This airy, light and homely restaurant/boutique hotel faces the Pittwater River side of Palm Beach, and the relaxed coastal vibe is the perfect accompaniment to light, Mediterranean fare. Tanned, relaxed 'Palmie' locals stroll by, stopping in for a quick coffee or a beer at the bar area adjacent to the brightly-lit dining room, which has vaulted ceilings and concertina doors that are usually thrown open to give the place a semi-outdoors atmosphere. You won't be seated in the prime street front seats unless you're eating a full meal, but the familial atmosphere inside is charming enough, with baskets of vine-ripened tomatoes, vases of flowers and shelves stacked with bottles of Italian mineral water. It's comfortable enough to spend an evening there, snuggled into one of the comfy armchairs strewn with blue-and-white striped cushions. The bar serves a small, thoughtful bar menu of *spuntini*-style snacks and antipasti, like a marinated seafood platter of chilled mussels, scallops, *vongole*, calamari, prawns and scampi with *fregola*, chilli and lemon dressing.

....

Beach Burrito *(bottom)*
252 Campbell Parade,
North Bondi
Tel: 02 9130 7123
www.beachburritocompany.com
Open: daily, 11am (8am Sat/Sun)–10pm

Casual, brightly-coloured and ultra laid-back, sandy feet are almost expected at this cheap and cheerful Mexican snack house. After a day in the sun, salt encrusted Bondi locals make a pilgrimage here, leaning their surfboards up against the wall outside and high-fiving

their mates who are already chowing down on tacos, quesadillas and the particularly moreish *tacitos* – which are scrummy baby corn tortillas packed with meat and cheese, and topped with lime juice, chilli and a dollop of guacamole, salsa or sour cream. On a hot summer's afternoon, it's a relaxed spot to pull up a chair and sink back a frozen margarita, brain freeze optional. If there's a few of you, BBC serves five coronas in a bucket of ice. *Ay Caramba!*

Bean Drinking *(left)*
Shop 1, 13 Ernest Place, Crows Nest
Tel: 02 9436 1678
www.beandrinking.com.au
Open: daily, 7am (8am Sat/Sun)–6pm

With plenty of outdoor seating, this personable café in the eat-and-shop precinct of Crows Nest is a god-send for North Shore coffee fiends, and the Coffee Lab is where caffeinated magic happens. Baristas here use a number of different brewing methods like cold drip, pour over and syphon, but what really impresses is the aptly-named Slayer espresso. This machine will thrill coffee junkies – it's one of only 40 in the world and it costs a whopping AU$26,000 because it allows the barista to manually control the machine's pressure. Whether it's Fairtrade or Rainforest Alliance, signs let you know exactly what you're drinking and where it comes from, and everything is roasted on-site in the Super Shop Roaster affectionately known as 'Monty.'

Bertoni Casalinga *(bottom)*
281 Darling Street, Balmain
Tel: 02 9818 5845
www.bertoni.com.au
Open: daily, 6.30am (7.30am Sun)
–6.30pm

Run by brothers Alberto and Antonio (Bert and Toni), Bertoni is a tiny hole-in-the-wall café that sits astride the bustling Darling Street, a famous strip of cafés and boutiques in the wealthy/boho suburb of Balmain. It's the kind of place to order an expertly-made coffee as you stroll past, unless, of course, you can snag yourself one of the bright red milk crates on the pavement. Made with a house blend of artisan beans, the coffee is superb and comes with a slice of almond biscotti on the side, and no matter how many they pump out, each comes with a genuine smile. As for the food, from lasagne to gnocchi, it's all homemade in a quintessential Italian trattoria-style, by Sicilian chef Claudio and the brothers' Naples-born mother, Mamma Maria. Everything is chalked up on the blackboard. Don't forget to try some *dolci* (Italian puddings), too.

Bills – Darlinghurst *(right)*
433 Liverpool Street, Darlinghurst
Tel: 02 9360 9631
www.bills.com.au
Open: daily, 7.30am (8.30am Sun)–3pm

It's safe to say nearly every Sydneysider has had breakfast at Bills, and the ones who haven't have at the very least heard of blonde celebrity chef Bill Grainger, who is affectionately dubbed Mr. Scrambled Eggs. His cafés do lunch, but breakfast is where it's at. Highlights include the

famed eggs, along with ricotta hotcakes smeared with fresh banana slices and honeycomb butter, and sweet corn fritters with roasted tomato, spinach and bacon. Those healthy fruit saladers won't find their bowl dominated by a massive amount of chopped apple, either. In Bill's mix, there's papaya, pineapple, melons, blood oranges and mandarins, served with a dollop of yoghurt and honey. It can get hectic in the morning, with gay couples, mums and prams and solo diners with their noses buried in newspapers. If the queues are too long, head to the other Bills in the chic, leafy 'burbs of nearby Woollahra (118 Queens Street, tel: 02 9328 7997) or Surry Hills (359 Crown Street, tel: 02 9360 4762).

Black Star *(top)*
277 Australia Street, Newtown
Tel: 02 9557 8656
www.blackstarpastry.com.au
Open: daily, 7am–5pm

If you haven't heard of a ginger ninja – get here fast. This playful bakery sells hundreds, if not thousands of the gingerbread biscuits to cafés across the city. Along with those, a calorific library of sweet treats awaits, like tartes tatins, strawberry, watermelon and rose cream cake, all the better when accompanied by the Little Marionette coffee. It's not the most spacious place to pitch up, however, with sugar junkies crammed onto the solo banquette lining the window, or squeezing themselves onto the few stools scattered about on the sidewalk – look out for the funky Philippe Starck gnome table. Aside from sugary bites, Black Star makes a mean quiche, sausage rolls and meat pies, and

being a bakery, the bread is top-notch. There's even a toast station, where you can pretend you're at a hotel breakfast buffet, and spread your slices with Vegemite, jam and all sorts.

Brasserie Bread Café *(middle)*
1737 Botany Road, Banksmeadow
Tel: 02 9666 8307
www.brasseriebread.com.au
Open: daily, 7am–3pm Mon–Fri;
8am–2pm Sat/Sun

It might be in a part of Sydney few would explore, but Brasserie Bread has developed something of a cult following for its carb-tastic bakery goods – particularly the caramelised garlic bread. Set next door to the bakery, the café and retail shop looks and smells inviting, with warehouse-style vaulted ceilings and tall pine shelves packed with artisan breads like organic sourdough, heavy rye and sour cherry loaf. It's the same artisan bread sold to hundreds of Sydney's cafés and restaurants, including many of the first-rate ones, and you can see for yourself what all the fuss is about as you munch on your croque monsieur because there's a glass-viewing gallery into the kitchen. It's a great little café with excellent coffee, and the devilishly-tasty sourdough pancakes, topped with stewed berry compote and honeycomb cream, are worth the trip alone. If you want to learn the tricks of the trade, it runs popular baking classes, too.

The Boathouse *(bottom)*
Palm Beach
Barrenjoey Boathouse, Governor Phillip Park, Palm Beach

snack...

171

Tel: 02 9974 3868
www.theboathousepb.com.au
Open: daily, 7.30am–4pm

A casual breakfast, lunch and drop-in café and provedore, The Boathouse is one of the northern beaches' most idyllic spots – be warned, you won't want to move once you park yourself on the timber deck, which suspends over Station Beach overlooking the tranquil Pittwater River. There's almost too much to gaze at while you soak up the sunshine on the deck – ferries chugging into the wharf, seaplanes skidding over the surface of the water, or dads and kids cramming into tinnies for fishing trips. As for food, head chef Leo Bressan serves up some of Sydney's best seafood – we can say with tried-and-tested authority that the beer-battered flathead fish and chips are exceptional, as are the green eggs and ham for brekkie – poached eggs, leg ham and heirloom tomatoes served atop crusty sourdough smeared with basil pesto.

Bondi FM Café & Bar (top)
143 Curlewis Street, Bondi Beach
Tel: 02 9130 6886;
www.bondifm.com.au
Open: 8am–11pm (10pm Sun). Closed Mondays.

Turn down an alley and follow the yellow-and-white thongs stencilled onto the ground to find this ultra laid-back café/bar belonging to Bondi 88.0 FM – the local community radio station. It's a super-casual beachside hangout with a house party-esque vibe, with an astro turf picnic area, old benches, worn sofas and graffiti-stencil murals on the walls. It attracts an equally laid-back clientele who lie in the sun on the grass nattering to mates, drinking coffee and scoffing bowls of buttered popcorn. There's more substantial snacks of sandwiches and pastas, and, being Bondi, a range of healthy salads, like brown rice and chick pea, falafel or tuna nicoise, along with thirst-quenching berry or mango smoothies served in old-school silver milkshake containers. It's licensed to sell booze, too, with Pimm's jugs and sangria the winners in summer, while in winter you can warm up with mulled wine. Try to get there during happy hour, between 5pm to 7pm during weekdays.

Bottega del Vino (bottom)
1/77 Macleay Street, Potts Point
Tel: 02 9331 8333
Open: daily, 10am–9pm (8pm Sat/Sun)

If you want cheese, wine, cured meats, or perhaps all of the above, then this glamorous little providore is a one-stop shop. It's a kid-in-a-candy-store moment for the gourmand – shelves are tightly packed with boutique olive oils, loaves of Sonoma artisanal bread and organic chocolate. The takeaway food, like homemade lasagna, plates of antipasti or a vegetarian pasta salad, has served many a local – picking up that night's dinner or something to take to a picnic lunch. As for vino, there are some fabulous choices, and solo imbibers need not fear – there's a handy range of 40 half-bottles from France, Italy, Australia and New Zealand. Grab one of those and a Ben and Jerry's ice-

Bondi FM
GARDEN

THE GARDEN IS A NON
SMOKING AREA...
IF YOU ARE CAUGHT SMOKING
YOU WILL BE ASKED TO LEAVE
SORRY IS NOT AN EXCUSE...
YOU CAN ALL READ THIS SIGN
AND IF YOU CANT YOUVE HAD
TOO MUCH TO DRINK AND
SHOULD GO SLEEP.

snack...

Shop 1 77 Macleay st

cream, and you'll be welcome at any picnic.

....

Bronte Road Bistro *(left)*
82 Bronte Road, Waverley
Tel: 02 9389 3028
www.bronteroadbistro.com
Open: noon–3pm Thurs–Sat,
6–10pm Tues–Sat

If you happen to be in the Eastern Beaches area – or power-walking along the famous Bondi to Bronte walk - take a (long) detour to the top of Bronte Road. A culinary powerhouse runs this neighbourly local bistro, with chef Dave Pegrum in the kitchen – he was once the head chef at Tetsuya's, and his finely-tuned French bistro classics are flawless. With a leafy courtyard, semi-al fresco glass atrium and a bright 'n' airy dining room, it's an excellent spot for a light meal. Order a glass (or two) of wine and snack on a basic Caprese salad or a chacuterie plate, with morsels of spicy calabrese salami, jamón serrano and creamy chicken liver pate. Make sure you order Iggy's bread, which is sourced from a nearby bakery with a cult-like following. The bistro encourages lingering, but there are a couple of bar stools to perch on if you just want a quick glass of wine and a bite at the eat-at bar.

....

Burnt Orange *(bottom)*
108 / 1109 Middle Head Road,
Mosman
Tel: 02 9969 1120
www.burntorange.com.au
Open: daily, 8.30am–5.30pm

Few Sydneysiders know about this little oasis, because it's tucked away in a secluded, harbourfront headland reserve. Set inside a beautifully restored sandstone golf club house from the 1930s, the café has a wide, wraparound verandah overlooking Sydney Harbour and the native bushland. If you head there for lunch try the famous fish pie, but be advised it's most renowned as a picturesque breakfast spot – with freshly-baked scones, huge bowls of organic porridge stewed with figs, prunes and a dollop of Riverina cream, spongy buttermilk pancakes and organic eggs and crispy bacon all on offer. The main dining room is warm and inviting, but the verandah is where you want to sit – most of the tables and their bright pink wooden chairs afford a view of the headland, harbour and native birds. If you'd rather sit on the lawns in front, the picnic kiosk can rustle up a picnic basket of takeaway salads and sandwiches.

....

Café Hernandez *(right)*
60 Kings Cross Road, Potts Point
Tel: 02 9331 2343
www.cafehernandez.com.au
Open: 24-hours daily

Spanish-born Joaquin Hernandez is an old-timer on Sydney's café scene – he's run this place since the 1970s and roasts his own coffee on-site. His Bohemian-style café is a tiny slip of a thing and off-the-radar to most Sydneysiders, but well-known to die-hard regulars, night owls and especially the cabbies, who can stop in for a caffeine fix at 4am. Furnished with shabby Victorian sofas, gorgeous paintings by Joa-

quin's late Barcelona-born wife Paquita Sabrafen and a polished antique coffee machine, there's a warmth to the place that has made it a neighbourhood institution. Joaquin's Spanish heritage translates to the menu, which features tortillas and chorizo rolls, and for a sweet fix, you can't not try the delectable *arroz con leche* (rice pudding).

 Café Giulia *(top)*
92 Abercrombie
Streer, Chippendale
Tel: 02 9698 4428 www.cafegiulia.com
Open: 6.30am–4pm Tues–Fri;
8am–3pm Sat/Sun

With its warehouses, urban gardens and fiercely proud city-dwellers, Chippendale is one of Sydney's coolest burgeoning inner-city suburbs, and Café Giula, set inside a converted 100-year-old corner butcher shop, fits in well. Step off the street and into the face of a gargantuan blackboard menu of pastries, sandwiches and salads, and friendly staff peeking out behind a coffee machine. There are benches and booths running along the narrow interior with a tiny shaded courtyard to the rear. This hip, urban oasis is hugely popular with trendy young design students from nearby University of Technology and the lucky owners of Chippendale's coveted warehouse apartments, and the coffee is brewed with love – as is the Moroccan tea with fresh mint, cloves and orange peel. Café fare comes in generous portions – think poached eggs and homemade hash browns for breakfast – and for lunch, sandwiches, salads and soups.

 Café Sopra *(left)*
Shop 8, 16 Hickson Road,
Walsh Bay
Tel: 02 8243 2700
www.fratellifresh.com.au
Open: noon–3pm, 6–10pm.
Closed Mondays.

Always abuzz, Café Sopra is the third Sydney café opened by the famous Italian greengrocer and providore Fratelli Fresh, and it's the best. The warehouse-style space sits opposite the wharf area of Woolloomooloo, with advertising agencies and theatregoers giving the place a trendy atmosphere. Get there well before your tummy starts rumbling because there are only a few tables outside on the pavement and the ones inside are nearly always full. There's nearly always a stool at the bright red mosaic *aperitivo* bar, which offers a daily selection of Italian beers, prosecco and freshly-made juices. As for the food, daily Italian specials are chalked up on a towering blackboard like ragu, fresh salads and antipasti snacks drizzled with fabulous extra virgin olive oil and aged balsamic vinegar. If you like what you're eating, Fratelli grocery products are on sale in the adjacent Vicino Casa di Fratelli.

Chargrill Charlies *(right)*
134 Queen Street, Woollahra
Tel: 02 9327 1008
www.chargrillcharlies.com.au
Open: daily, 9am–9pm

Don't be fooled into thinking this is some ordinary John Doe chicken shop. Chargrill Charlies is an institution, and to work it out, you only need to look at

snack...

the wall of photographs documenting all of the celebrities who have stopped by for the epic grainfed barbecue chooks. Everyone from Russell Crowe, Nicole Kidman and Oprah Winfrey have walked these hallowed grounds, ordered their food and posed for a happy snap with the grinning owners. The famous chicken in question is crucified and roasted on a mega rotisserie, then served with a mountain of salty fries, or any one of the healthy salads on display behind the counter glass. It's soul food, and even better if you have a hangover like an axe to the head – any Australian will tell you that barbecue chicken has miraculous hangover curing properties, especially when washed down with a beer.

Leading the Waterloo revolution, which saw a rather derelict suburb transform into one of Sydney's chic urban nooks, Danks Street Depot sits alongside galleries, gourmet grocers and vintage stores. Chef Jarad Ingersoll runs this incredibly popular warehouse-style café basing the seasonal menu on the principles of the slow-food movement. There's always an eccentric, interesting crowd stopping off for lunch after perusing the nearby galleries, so you might have to wait for one of the bar stools, which sit astride long wooden bars. Try the hot, braised beef and caramelised onion sandwich, served on schiacatta with crispy Chat potatoes.

 Danks Street Depot   *(left)*
2-6 Danks Street, Waterloo
Tel: 02 9319 4420
www.danksstdepot.com.au
Open: daily, 7.30am (8am Sat, 9am Sun)–4pm (11pm Thurs–Sat)

Deus ex Machina   *(middle)*
98-104 Parramatta Road, Camperdown
Tel: 02 9519 3669
www.deus.com.au
Open: daily, 7am–3.30pm; 6pm–late Weds–Sat

178

snack...

If you've ever lusted after Harleys and Yamahas, Deus ex Machina (meaning 'god from a machine' in Latin) is your café. It's almost motorcycle porn, sipping espresso and munching on fruit toast while ogling at the bike of your dreams in the attached Deus showroom. With high ceilings, tall wooden beams and funky murals adorning the walls, the airy café has oversized communal teak tables and wicker sofas to curl up in, ciabatta sandwich in one hand and motorcycle mag in the other. The lovers of hard and fast bikes will love the place, which sells custom bikes with names like Deus Grievous Angel to Kawasakis and more – including vintage motorcycle paraphernalia and gear. A well-oiled fantasy.

Detour Espresso Bar *(right)*
Shop 4a, 135 – 143 William Street, Darlinghurst
Tel: 02 4507 60841
www.detourcafe.com.au

Open: daily, 7am (8am Sat / Sun)–5pm (2pm Sat / Sun)

There's some seriously good coffee brewing at Detour. This funky hole-in-the-wall café is right on William Street, an arterial road linking the city to Kings Cross, but no one seems to care about the noisy traffic lumbering past. There's nearly always a bunch of people from locals, commuters on their way to work and even teens from nearby SCEGGS college waiting patiently on the sidewalk for coffee and chatting to staff. The friendliness of this café is one of the highlights – all members of staff are personable and will happily bring you a glass of water while you wait. Grab a seat on one of the wooden crates beside low tables on the pavement, or perch on the pine wood benches running the length of the room inside. Coffee is the main focus, but Detour does a mean fresh mango smoothie, with rolls, paninis, wraps and salads all on offer for lunch.

179

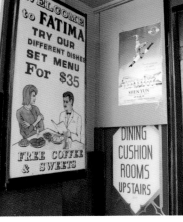

Eathouse Diner *(top)*
306 Chalmers Street, Redfern
Tel: 02 8084 9479
Open: noon (10am Sat/Sun)–10pm
(3pm Sun). Closed Mondays.

The turquoise and scarlet painted entrance and gigantic mural of a monster bird is well-suited to Eathouse, a warm yet on-the-pulse diner run by three young friends – two chefs and a stylist. There's lots to like about it, like big windows and miscellaneous stuff like bull horns, retro lampshades and naughty newspaper clippings plastered over the bathroom walls, as well as super attentive service. The open kitchen pumps out a steady stream of bistro-style cuisine; think duck-liver pâté, pork-laden Waldorf salad, poached chicken sandwich and a massive banana to take you back to your childhood. It's nearly always busy with a young, hipster crowd, and it's an easygoing place to kick back for an unhurried evening feed.

Fatima's *(left)*
294-296 Cleveland Street,
Surry Hills
Tel: 02 9698 4895
Open: daily, 9am–3am

When you've quaffed one too many cocktails and have a hankering for a late-night falafel, Fatima is your lady. This late-night trading Lebanese restaurant has one of the busiest takeaway counters in Sydney, serving traditional Lebanese food until 3am every day. From crunchy-on-the-outside and mushy-on-the-inside *kibbe* and falafel, to delicious cabbage rolls, smooth hummus drizzled with olive oil and coarsely-chopped *tabouleh*, it's all wrappable in freshly-baked Lebanese bread. The basic takeaway counter with its low-lit fluorescent lighting suffices for a taxi pit-stop (every cabbie will know it), but if you want to kick back head upstairs to the cushion rooms, where a belly dancer wobbles her hips salaciously on Friday and Saturday nights.

Flat White *(right)*
98 Holdsworth Street (corner
of Jersey Road), Woollahra
Tel: 02 9328 9922
Open: daily, 7am (8am Sun)–4pm

In the well-to-do suburb of Woollahra, directly opposite the charming Lord Dudley pub (see Drink), this unassuming little café does a roaring neighbourhood trade, attracting a mix of residents and art-lovers popping in to check out the area's galleries, including the one upstairs. While it may look ordinary, Flat White has a slew of regulars who keep coming back for the pork sandwich. With its crunchy crackling and crisp apple, chutney and rocket, it's a blockbuster. It's only matched somewhat by the seven-hour lamb sandwich, with its sweet caramelised onions and 'nana's relish', a fragrant mix of vinegar, cumin, paprika and mustard powder. There's another coup – breakfast is served all day long and the fresh juices are delish. Grab some counter space along the open windows and enjoy.

snack...

Forbes & Burton *(left)*
252 Forbes Street (corner of Burton), Darlinghurst
Tel: 02 9356 8788
www.forbesandburton.com.au
Open: daily, 7am (8am Sat/Sun)–4pm

Effortlessly hip, casual and proudly eco, Forbes & Burton is set in a beautiful corner heritage building with sandstone walls and hardwood floors, low benches along the window and a few outdoor tables. Always pumping, it seems to be a Mecca for the Eastern Suburbs' creative types who show up with their Mac laptops and design sketch pads and leave several hours and numerous Fairtrade macchiatos later. F&B does a roaring trade in bacon and egg rolls, with caramelised onion, *croque monsieurs* and *madames* for breakfast, while at lunch plates like vegetarian chickpea falafel panini with *babaganoush* and harissa yoghurt are filling and excellent value. There's also gluten-free meals and free WiFi, though electrical sockets are frustratingly absent.

Four Ate Five *(top)*
485 Crown Street, Surry Hills
Tel: 02 9698 6485
Open: daily, 7am (7.30am Sat, 9.30am Sun)–4.30pm (2.30pm Sun)

Quirky and casual, this is a great little café fronting the hubbub of hip Crown Street, attracting a steady stream of fashionable young locals with their signature Macbook or skateboard tucked under their arms. The café's Moroccan-baked eggs with *labne* and flaked almonds are among the best in town – served with hunks of fresh sourdough perfect for dunking. Whether you feel like healthy bircher muesli or whacking on the kilojules early in the day with the whopper Mexican breakfast – a giant mound of beans, salsa and fried eggs and topped with crispy bacon, there's lots to choose from. It's a casual little place with lots of fun touches. Order a peppermint tea, for example, and you'll get a glass of hot water stuffed to the brim with fresh mint leaves and a plastic toy gun filled with honey to squirt yourself.

Gertrude and Alice *(right)*
46 Hall Street, Bondi Beach
Tel: 02 9130 5155
www.gertrudeandalice.com.au
Open: daily, 7.15am–10pm

Bookish types, hippies, lesbian couples and layabouts all love this beachside bookshop café, which has perfected its chill-out-you're-in-Bondi vibe. Only a hop, skip and meander from the sands, there are worse ways to spend a Sunday than here, parked on a bench outside – newspaper spread on the table, and munching a blueberry bagel or scrumptious bircher muesli topped with rhubarb and yoghurt. The café is also famous for its steaming pots of Chai tea. If you too become enamoured, you can buy packets of it behind the counter, along with an interesting range of second-hand books. Allow yourself some time to savour the shelves and pick up a vintage Penguin classic or a well-thumbed Hemingway.

snack...

Gusto *(left)*
2a Heely Street, Paddington
Five Ways
Tel: 02 9361 5640
Open: daily, 7am–8pm

A place to preen and be seen, Gusto is perennially chock full of fashionable Paddington residents, and is, many would say, the heart of the little village known as Five Ways. The point where five streets culminate, it's a buzzy little area lined with Victorian terraces, pubs, independent art galleries and Sydney's cream-of-the-crop fashion boutiques. Set to one corner of the roundabout, the delicatessen-slash-café has a cluster of tables on the sidewalk, prime real estate for a spot of people-watching. It's loved by locals, gallery-owners and designers who flock here for weekend breakfasts and strong coffee in the sun. Lunchtime snacks are equally as home-style and direct from the Italian deli,

with toasted paninis, foccacias, leafy salads, cured meats and a naughty range of *dolci* sweets to nibble on with a soy latte.

 Harry's Café *(middle)*
de Wheels
Corner Cowper Wharf Roadway &
Brougham Road, Woolloomooloo
Tel: 02 9357 3074
Open: daily, 8.30am–2am (3am Weds/
Thurs, 4am Fri/Sat, 1am Sun)

If eating a pie is a religious experience, then Harry's is the Vatican. Scoffing down a 'tiger' meat pie piled with mushy peas, creamy mash and neon-stewed gravy is not only a religion to most Sydneysiders, it's more Australian than kangaroos, koalas and Vegemite combined. Michael Hannah's old cart sits alongside the wharf, and has sold pies since the 1930s when the city

council insisted that mobile food caravans move a minimum of 12 inches a day. From selling pies to wharfies and sailors, the celebrities who have visited over the past 70-odd years reads like a red carpet who's-who list, and the walls of the caravan are plastered with their photos to prove it. From Elton John and Frank Sinatra to Brook Shields and Anthony Bourdain – they've all eaten a pie here, and so should you. Don't deny yourself the unadulterated pleasure of sitting wharfside after a night out in the city, listening to the seagulls and chowing down a 'tiger'. It's a must.

Jackie's *(right)*
122 Oxford Street (corner of Glenmore Road), Paddington
Tel: 02 9380 9818
Open: daily, 8am–10pm

Don your finest threads and your darkest Prada sunglasses because this is where the fashion set do lunch. Set in a split courtyard with direct access to hip Paddington fashion boutiques, Jackie's is as much about being seen as it is about shopping-pit-stop-lunching. If it's a sunny day, the tables on the terrace are swarming with well-heeled regulars, while the lower level has a smattering of intimate tables away from prying eyes. There's also another section adjacent to the courtyard; an eat-at sushi bar where you can prop up, swill Champagne and nibble on sashimi after busting your credit card at the chic boutiques along Glenmore Road. As well as sushi, the fare is café-style – the huge, leafy sashimi salad and steak sandwich are the highlights.

snack…

Latteria *(left)*
320 Victoria Street, Darlinghurst
Tel: 02 9331 2914
Open: daily, 5am–7pm

Latteria has one of the best people-watching perches on buzzy Victoria Street, which links the eclectic suburb of Darlinghurst with its naughty Kings Cross sibling. The passing parade is a mix of hipsters, Eastern Suburbs gastronomes, pimps and wild-eyed hobos – even during the light of day. There's scarcely room to swig an espresso in the slender interior, which is as narrow as a corridor and features a counter along one side and small scattered tables on the other. Instead, pull up one of the wooden stools on the pavement where Darlo old-timers set up shop, and sup a Segafredo cappuccino with your newspaper. Don't expect an array of gourmet treats; food-wise, it's simple foccacias and paninis all around.

Little Ethel's *(right)*
84 Mullens Street, Balmain
Tel: 02 9555 9911
Open: daily, 6.30am–4.30pm Mon–Sat;
7am–2pm Sun

It's so tacky it's cool. Garden party-style retro tables and chairs atop a carpet of artificial grass, colourful gnomes and a white picket fence. This quirky little café is named after shop-owner Jamie Woolcott's granny, and it's already one of Balmain's most popular – quite a feat for a suburb bursting at the seams with choices. Food includes scrumptious scrambled eggs, sandwiches and pastries, and potent coffee brewed with Single Origin beans. Queues can snake out the door in the breakfast rush – if you manage to grab one of the few tables, order the thick slices of toasted sourdough with avocado, mushrooms, tomato, onion and basil.

Little Marionette in Balmain *(middle)*
1a Booth Street, Balmain
Tel: 02 9810 9728
www.thelittlemarionette.com
Open: daily, 6.30am (7am Sat,
8am Sun)–4pm

Self-described coffee nerds; Little Marionette is a miniscule café in Balmain that pumps out caffeine dreams and sells their beans wholesale to a slew of other Sydney cafés. It's so tiny there's rare hope of snagging a seat, but fear not – the waitstaff will happily bring your coffee across the road to the park, so pull up some grass. If you do snare some bum space on the cushy Chesterfield sofa, don't rush away in a hurry. Order yourself a double ristretto piccolo and be won over by friendly service, panini-style sandwiches and soft chunks of freshly-baked banana bread.

Miss Chu *(bottom)*
150 Bourke Street (near the corner
of William Street), Darlinghurst
Tel: 02 8356 9988
www.misschu.com.au
Open: 11am–9pm Mon–Fri

Part-canteen, part-hawker stall-meets-tuck shop, Miss Chu claims to make the best Vietnamese rice paper rolls in town and she's not wrong. Along with those, Miss Chu serves up fabulous

187

dumplings, duck pancakes, vermicelli noodle salads and steamed *char sui* pork BBQ buns, which are out of this world. Everything is whipped up in the kitchen and passed out the window in quaint takeaway bags and Asian paper boxes. It's an eclectic little place and hugely popular with the funky Darlinghurst hipsters – snaring one of the wooden stools and crates scattered over the pavement proves near-impossible on a busy lunchtime day. All orders need to be placed at the window, framed by brightly-coloured paper lanterns and the constant beats of Miss Chu's own CD compilation, available to purchase. Miss Chu also delivers within a one-kilometre radius on G-force electric bikes – worth keeping in mind if you're staying in Darlinghurst or Potts Point and have a hankering for pork buns.

 Le Monde *(top)*
83 Foveaux Street, Surry Hills
Tel: 02 9211 3568
Open: 6.30am–4pm Mon–Fri;
7am–2pm Sat

The flow of coffee is so fast and furious here that sweaty-browed baristas can scarcely glance up at the chic slew of locals lining up at the counter, which is a good sign for serious coffee-lovers. The global beans (Ethiopian, Sumatran, Bolivian, Tanzanian – you name it) and brewing methods at Le Monde are both exceptional, though the queues in the morning may put off non-believers. To the right of the devoted, usually crowded around the coffee dispensary, is an airy, pleasant dining area, with tables and chairs looking out onto the slope of Foveaux Street. Scrambled eggs or the deconstructed BLAT are breakfast winners, while lunch menu items like salads, pastas et al are chalked up on the blackboard. True coffee nuts may want to try the three-course breakfast degustation menus matched with coffee, although prepare to bounce off walls the remainder of the day.

 Nielsen Park *(bottom)*
Café Kiosk
Nielsen Park, Greycliffe Avenue, Vaucluse
Tel: 02 9337 7333
www.nielsenpark.com.au
Open: daily, 8am–4pm

With its shaded thicket of trees and grassy slopes, the beautiful Nielsen Park cradles one of Sydney's most stunning harbour beaches, and as the only café in the area, this charming beach house-style kiosk is hugely popular – particularly in the height of summer when the place heaves with barefoot, sand-encrusted beachgoers. The safe waters and netted swimming area means the place is teeming with young families, but if you don't mind the occasional piercing screech of a toddler, the sparkling view of the harbour is one of Sydney's loveliest. Smack-bang on the beach promenade, the casual kiosk pumps out coffees, takeaway snacks and no-frills fare, and to the left is the café. Set inside a bright, restored pavilion with original stained-glass windows and hardwood floors, it serves a heavenly breakfast; think runny eggs benedict with portobello mushrooms or homemade granola with creamy yoghurt. When breakfast winds up chef Daniel Hughes serves light Mediterra-

MORNIN

ALL D

snack...

nean fare – graze on a tasting plate for two, with herb-crusted prawn cutlets, duck liver pâté and panzanella salad. It's one of Sydney's most idyllic secret harbour beach hideaways. Bring along a beach towel and a book for later, because you won't want to leave.

Olio Mediterranean Brasserie *(top)*
205 Pacific Highway, St. Leonards
Tel: 02 9439 8988
www.olio.com.au
Open: 7am–9pm (4pm Mon).
Closed Saturdays and Sundays.

Java snobs will sniff that this is one of the only places in Sydney that stocks the exclusive kop luwak coffee from Indonesia which has, in essence, passed through the rear end of a tree climbing-cat known as a civet. After passing through undigested with the fleshy coating removed, it's thankfully washed and then roasted. Served on an elegant slate platter at AU$9 a cup, it's possibly up there among the world's most expensive brews, but North Shore coffee-lovers happily part with the cash. It's not the only brew here at Olio – there's another organic coffee blend formulated exclusively for the brassiere by award-winning roasters. Olio isn't just about coffee, either – it's a casual though elegant trattoria-style eatery serving light Italian food. The coffee might be the excuse to visit, but the brassiere also excels at light meals like lentil salad with beetroot, asparagus, goat's cheese and sherry vinegar or soft salmon and potato fish cakes, served with shaved fennel, radish and lemon aioli.

Plan B *(middle)*

204 Clarence Street, CBD
Tel: 02 9283 3450
www.becasse.com.au
Open: 8am–4pm Mon–Fri

A side project of celebrated chef Justin North, Plan B sits astride the elegant Becasse restaurant in the middle of the Sydney CBD, a cleverly-placed hole in the wall café that churns out expertly-made Single Origin coffee and serves one of Sydney's best (and cheapest) Wagyu burgers, featuring 600-day Gundooee organic grass-fed beef, caramelised onions and beetroot. At a paltry AU$10 (you read it right), the burger, along with sausage rolls encased in crusty yet flaky pastry, muffins and freshly-packed sandwiches and salads, make Plan B massively popular among time-poor, well-heeled city executives. It's a welcome respite from the stodgy city eateries in the CBD and a great chance to sample well-priced food presided over by one of Sydney's most respected chefs.

Poolside Cafe *(bottom)*
Andrew Boy Charlton Pool, 1C
Mrs. Macquarie's Road, The Domain
Tel: 02 8354 1044
www.poolsidecafe.com.au
Open: dail,y 7.30am–4pm

Overlooking the eight-lane, 50-metre Andrew Boy Charlton swimming pool and Woolloomooloo Bay, the Poolside Café has floor-to-ceiling views from the sparkling harbour to the Domain gardens. The café opens out onto a sunny terrace where you can top up your tan in a rattan chair or perve at the bronzed

snack...

191

bodies sunning themselves below. The food is light, fresh and perfect for a post-dip snack – like soft-flour tortilla with tomato coriander salsa and deep sea bream and prosciutto salad with grilled peaches and buffalo mozzarella, washed down with a chilled pinot gris or an espresso. The clientele is made up of mostly swimmers, and as the pool attracts a large gay community, you should expect some seriously buff, impeccably-groomed men sauntering around in miniscule swimmers.

 Porch & Parlour Bondi *(bottom)*
100-102 Brighton Boulevard,
North Bondi
Tel: 02 9300 0111
www.porchandparlour.com.au
Open: daily, 7am–6pm

Porch is a shop, a cool retail space selling retro push bikes, Penguin classics, clothing brands like Skinny Nelson, organic t-shirts and bespoke jewellery pieces by Metallic Dreamer. The Parlour is the café, a casual eatery with a jumble of second-hand furniture finds spilling out onto the plant-strewn pavement. It's rancho relaxo for post-Vinyasa yoga class hipsters, who sip soy lattes and chow down the café's signature 'smashed egg' dish of hardboiled free-range eggs rolled in basil and salt and served with slices of avocado and toast. Java snobs might not rate the coffee as highly, but there's a good range of juices and smoothies and the food is hearty and healthy, like frittatas, crusty linseed and soy sandwiches and falafel, tomatoes, cucumber and mint salad doused with lashings of yoghurt dressing.

La Renaissance *(left)*
Café Patisserie
47 Argyle Street, The Rocks
Tel: 02 9241 4878
www.larenaissance.com.au
Open: daily, 8am–6pm

This charming French patisserie has been serving Sydney's most exquisite macaron and croissants to discerning city folk for more than three decades. Owned by the Charkos family, who also run Baroque Bistro a few blocks nearby, La Renaissance is set inside a historic sandstone building and carries on the legacy of the late family patriarch, Parisian-born chef Pierre Charkos. Valrhona chocolate is used exclusively in all the cakes and pastries here, and as well as éclairs, tarts and towering crocembouche, the patisserie has a sweet little garden courtyard to the rear, where you can sup brilliant coffee and order from the lunch menu, which features homemade meat pies, quiche and tasty baguettes. Prepare to queue in the morning – this place makes a mean macchiato, and locals know it.

 Ripples *(right)*
Deck C, Chowder Bay Road,
Mosman
Tel: 02 9960 3000
www.aquadining.com.au
Open: daily, 8–10.30am Sat/Sun, noon–3pm (4pm Sat/Sun),6–9.30pm (9pm Sun)

Ripples makes the perfect pit-stop between walking along the Sydney harbour foreshore from Taronga Zoo to Balmoral Beach – even better if you want to spend the day horizontal at Clifton Gardens, one of Sydney's

snack...

most secluded harbour beaches (arrive in style via water taxi from Circular Quay). With glittering views over the harbour, Ripples also serves lunch and dinner, but it shines at breakfast on weekends, when the al fresco terrace heaves with relaxed locals. There are no reservations – strictly walk-ins only – but gazing at the view, you won't worry too much if you have to wait. Try the porridge served with rhubarb compote and lashings of brown sugar or the fluffy Kangaroo Valley egg omelette.

....

Remy and Lee's (left)
547 Bourke Street, Surry Hills
Tel: 02 4033 61400
Open: 7am (8am Sun)–4pm.
Closed Mondays.

There's a cycling craze in Sydney and bike-loving hipsters can't get enough of this cute little café, which is right on pedal-friendly Bourke Street and equipped with an on-site pump and other cycle bits and pieces, displayed in cabinets along with trinkets and Buddha statues. There's a communal table taking up most of the café, and the whimsical hipster crowd is happy with the bums-on-milk-crates seating arrangements. Food includes a yummy bircher muesli and sourdough toast sandwiches, though muffins are the speciality; expect them in quirky flavour combinations such as Vegemite and cheese, peanut butter and jam, all washed down with coffee from Sydney roastery Little Marionette. Other pastry items and sweet treats are sourced from Newtown's Black Star bakery.

....

Single Origin (middle)
60-64 Reservoir Street, Surry Hills
Tel: 02 9211 0665
www.singleoriginroasters.com.au
Open: 6.30am–4pm Mon–Fri

This is not the place to utter the words 'decaffeinated soy caramel latte'. These guys are serious about their beans, so be aware that you're ordering

your espresso from bonafide coffee-meisters. The coffee comes from the roastery in the suburb of Alexandria, but you can sample the good stuff at the Single Origin café as you please – espresso, syphon, pour over or cold filter. There's a café menu, and while the salads and sandwiches (think miso-glazed lamb, Japanese eggplant and asparagus, and the housemade nutella sandwich with banana) will rock your boat too, the real reason this place is famous is for the global range of pre-mium-grade, sustainably-grown coffee. It's so popular that the owners recently added Sideshow – a takeaway espresso bar next door – to reduce the madness of the morning caffeine rush.

Shortlist *(right)*
258 Abercrombie Street, Darlington
Tel: 02 4226 43768
www.theshortlistespresso.com
Open: daily, 7am (8am Sat,
9am Sun)–4pm (3pm Sun)

Tucked in a street-front terrace in an eclectic inner-city suburb surrounded by converted warehouse apartments, hidden art galleries and grungy university student digs, The Shortlist attracts alternative, inner-city clientele and the vibe is ultra-relaxed. Grab a spot on the sturdy wooden communal table inside or a perch on a wooden stool and crate on the pavement to sup espresso, organic juice or an icy apple, berry and yoghurt frappe. If you're peckish, food items (and witty quips) are chalked up on the blackboard. Tuck into home-style snacks like avocado on thick slices of sourdough, served with SP sauce and lemon oil, baked beans with *bocconcini* and chorizo or homemade muesli. The café sources most of its stock from Sydney suppliers – the fabulous array of pastries and sweets come courtesy of Black Star bakery in Newtown, while the coffee is from Balmain's Little Marionette.

195

 Tea Parlour *(left)*
569 Elizabeth Street,
Redfern
Tel: 02 4143 35224
Open: 1–8pm Weds–Sun

Bring out your genteel side at this quirky streetside sitting room, which has been inventively appointed by owner Amelia with thrift-store finds, including lace tablecloths, restored Victorian sofas, mismatched vases and a gloriously-feathered taxidermy peacock. Served on silver platters with soft, fluffy scones smothered with jam and cream, the high tea is the highlight (pun fully intended) at Tea Parlour which serves more than twenty varieties like Earl Grey, peppermint and Devonshire to Mongolian herb, Wuyi Rock and Quince Green. As well as tea, there are snacky plates of cucumber and ham sandwiches. It's a beautifully-appointed parlour – the sultry jazz tunes playing in the background are the icing on the cake.

 Toby's Estate *(middle)*
2-36 City Road, (between
Broadway and Myrtle Streets,
opposite Victoria Park) Chippendale
Tel: 02 9211 1459
www.tobysestate.com.au
Open: 7am–4pm Mon–Fri

As well as supplying several hundred cafés around NSW with their coffee, there are numerous Toby's cafés scattered around in Woolloomooloo, Potts Point and Bondi Junction, but this one opposite the rolling lawns of Victoria Park is one of the best. It's a welcoming spot and nearly always overrun with university students from nearby University of Sydney. The house espresso blend is rich, warm, chocolately and almost too easy to drink with

everything from Ethiopia Harar and Sidamo to Brazil Daterra and Costa Rica Tarrazu La Pastora to whet the coffee-lover's appetite. With glass windows overlooking the street, the café interior has shelves packed with coffee beans, hessian sacks, jars of tea and coffee paraphernalia, while the counter sells a range of tasty quiches, muffins and sandwiches ready to eat – try the bacon and egg roll with hollandaise sauce.

Tropicana Caffe *(right)*
Shop 1, 227 Victoria Street, Darlinghurst
Tel: 02 9360 9809
www.tropicanacaffe.com
Open: daily, 5am–10.30pm

An institution in Sydney, Tropicana Caffe is at the core of the beating heart of Darlinghurst, where gays, straights, pimps and strippers come to read newspapers, drink coffee and preen in full view of passing Kings Cross traffic. 'The Trop', as it's known, is more than just a café, it's the place where Australia's largest amateur short film competition, Tropfest, began – back when only a few films were screened in the café. These days it's well-loved and renowned for simple home-style cuisine like minestrone soup or the legendary Trop salad, a mammoth mix of crispy cos lettuce and rocket topped with a hardboiled egg, sun-dried tomatoes, grilled vegetables and tuna. Service is at the basic end, but it means well –order at the counter, find a seat on the sidewalk and enjoy the show.

party…

Nightclubs in Sydney lean two ways – they're either filled with glamouristas, gaunt models and men with an unhealthy interest in their own reflection, or it's a get-sweaty-on-the-dance floor situation with addictive beats and a carefree, up-for-it crowd.

Most of the city's clubs, much to the delight of Sydney's police, are concentrated in the red light district of Kings Cross, where lingerie-clad ladies swirl around the poles at strip clubs sandwiched along one main drag known as 'The Golden Mile'. With its sleazy hustlers, marauding stag parties and revved-up cars cruising the streets, The Cross might be Sydney's most risqué area but it's a whole lot more genteel than it was during the 1980s, when you couldn't walk two steps without running into a drug dealer, a prostitute or a corrupt cop – perhaps all three at once. These days, the surrounding streets beneath the neon Coca-Cola sign at the top of William Street are packed with expensive apartments, upmarket cocktail bars, cafés, nightclubs and restaurants. With so many clubs within a few metres of each other, it's all too easy to lurch from cocktail bar to nightclub, to cocktail bar and maybe another nightclub, without any trouble from the riff-raff. Here we've listed the best choices in the area.

As for making it past the velvet ropes? Rather sadly there are regular whinings about beefy nightclub doormen refusing entry to the occasional gentleman deemed unworthy. Put simply, you're at their mercy, and if you don't make an effort with your gladrags, are too boozed-up or give them any lip, expect to hear 'not tonight' or 'guest-list only'. Best to be patient and unfailingly polite, bring along a foxy wingwoman or try phoning or emailing the club a few days in advance to get your name on the guest-list.

Once you're inside, what to expect? Taking its cue from the British scene, Sydney's clubbing has always been infatuated with beat-friendly, lyric-driven house, though as it matured from the ecstasy phase it's become more common to find pop, hip-hop, R&B and indie-friendly clubs that feature bands as well as DJs. Keep an eye out for electro-driven, techno-inspired Bang Gang DJs, electro-pop-dance group Sneaky Sound System, any Future Classic events and check www.threedworld. com.au or www.inthemix.com.au for all nightclubbing news and events.

No matter the venue, clubbers tend to be a friendly bunch and they dress to impress – ladies clip-clopping around in stilettos and miniskirts in slicker venues like Tank, The Tunnel, Ivy and Ladylux, while at Chinese Laundry, Melt, Home and Kit & Kaboodle it's toned down to the fashion-forward, hipster end of the spectrum. Men need to up the fashion ante to get past the clipboards – wearing sneakers or trainers, even those Nike Limited Edition Air Force Ones – won't cut the mustard. However, you can wear whatever you like while partying hard at any one of the city's music festivals, day-long shenanigans when Sydneysiders really let their hair down. Luring international bands and DJ big-wigs, the cream of the crop are Good Vibrations, Field Day, Big Day Out, Parklife, Future Music Festival and Harbourlife (check www.fuzzy.com.au and www.jammusic.com.au for details).

CLUBS

Arq *(left)*
16 Flinders Street, Darlinghurst
Tel: 02 9380 8700
www.arqsydney.com.au
Open: 9.30pm–late Thurs–Sun

Three-dimensional lasers and lights, high-energy handbag house and trance; this is Sydney's best gay nightclub and it has the whole shebang if you want to sweat and grind it up on the dance floor into the wee hours of the morning. It's a rambling space with a central stage where gender-bending diva drag queens perform on Thursdays and Sundays, a large dance floor area, two bars and VIP areas. Always busy, Arq clubbers like to put on the razzle-dazzle when they head out, so expect lots of buff, superbly-groomed gay men with well-oiled bare chests, miniscule hot pants and the like. But don't worry if you don't fit the mould or even if you're a straighty 180 – Arq clubbers are exceedingly friendly and suitably juiced with potent cocktails (the kind you don't buy from the bartender, if you catch our drift).

Candy's Apartment *(right)*
22 Bayswater Road, Kings Cross
Tel: 02 9380 5600
www.candys.com.au
Open: 10pm–late Fri & Sat

Formerly Zen, China White and the Underground, the club beneath this Bayswater Road terrace is now known as Candy's Apartment. It opens during the weekend, with clubbers spilling outside onto Bayswater Road amid the less salubrious Kings Cross flotsam and jetsam. The interiors are moody and low ceilings give the place a subterranean feel, with exposed brick archways and banquettes if you want to sit and have a shouting tête-à-tête with other clubbers. It's a bit of a mish-mash when it comes to DJs – everything from house to disco, bands and international DJs and groups like the Presets, Wolfmother and Valentinos play here, either in the front room or the smaller back room. Bear in mind it's the Cross, so slap on an angelic face and be on your best behaviour when you walk up to the door. The stony-faced doormen put up with a lot of shtick, and there's no telling whether they will like the look of you.

Chinese Laundry *(bottom)*
Corner of King and Sussex Streets
Tel: 02 8295 9950
www.jammusic.com.au
Open: 10pm–late Fri & Sat

Ranked number one club in Australia in DJ Mag's 'Top 100 Clubs in the World' poll, the Laundry's three sweaty club rooms make for one massive party playground. The age of revellers may make third-decade clubbers feel wrinkles forming on the spot, but it's one of the best clubbing experiences in the city. Set beneath Slip Inn bar, there are three rooms with ornate statues and Chinese-inspired interiors, and the place gets crammed come Friday and Saturday nights. A host of international names have spun the decks here, from Timo Maas and Krafty Kuts to Stacey Pullen – expect to boogie to house, electro, tech, progressive and breaks.

party...

Try to get here for one of its infamous garden parties when the outdoor terrace area heaves with people, but be prepared to pay up – basic entry costs AU$20.

The Club (top)
33 Bayswater Road, Kings Cross
Tel: 02 9331 0511
www.theclubsydney.com
Open: 10pm–late Fri & Sat

If you can bear crotchety doormen and the steep price of drinks, The Club is a rollicking spot for nocturnal shenanigans – especially if you detest dance music yet yearn for a club environment, as DJs play a mixture of Jay Z and Guns 'n' Roses, with everything from Britpop to Blondie blasting out of the speakers. The actual club itself has a scarlet history – it was once a former strip club known as Dancers Cabaret and the pole stage is still there and successfully continues to entice many a tipsy gaggle of girls. There's a main dance area, a medley of sofas and potted plants and an outdoor patio area out the front, with various private areas to hire out if you want to lord it up (of course you do!) on plush Chesterfield sofas, with bottles of Belvedere vodka on ice and exclusive bar service from waitresses – they can even arrange a private DJ if you show 'em the money. Reserve the Bat Cave, a private room just to the side near the DJ, which has a key-pad code for guests and an exclusive bar and floor team catering to your every whim.

Favela (middle)
1 Kellet Way, Potts Point
Tel: 02 9357 1640
www.favela.com.au
Open: Thurs–Sat, dinner seatings at 7pm & 9pm

It's named after a Brazilian slum but Favela is a nudge or two classier – it's a Brazilian bar and restaurant that transforms later in the evening into a glam nightclub. Get there early for a *churrasco*, barbecued meats roasted on skewers, and knock back zesty caipirinhas until the kitchen closes and the club action begins. If you do that, it means your booth-style seating becomes your own private party den for the evening, meaning no queues, no fuss to get in and no extra cost. Thursdays host acoustic nights, with soulful musos twanging on guitars, while the get-down-and-dirty clubbing fun takes over on weekends, with house DJs spinning tunes on a Funktion 1 sound system on the weekly Saturday HedKandi nights. The main room is where the friendly, party-hearty crowd busts out the moves, but the revellery spreads over two levels. There are private lounges, including one covered wall-to-wall with gold tiles. Don't forget to head upstairs to dance under a ceiling covered with pulsating lights.

Greenwood Hotel (bottom)
36 Blue Street, North Sydney
Tel: 02 9964 9477
www.greenwoodhotel.com
Open: daily, from 5pm

It may be north of the bridge and in the midst of an otherwise dull business district, but the Greenwood Ho-

tel has seduced clubbers from all over Sydney for years – hosting some of the biggest-name DJs and the iconic former Sounds on Sunday parties. Those Sunday shenanigans finished a while ago, but the Greenie still pulls the crowds for special events like Twilight Sounds, Sounds on Boxing Day or Sounds on New Year's Day. If you manage to get to one of these you won't be disappointed. It's an impressive venue – set inside a restored former school (and chapel) with gorgeous sandstone walls and a huge outdoor area framed by the surrounding high-rise buildings. There are four bars, drinks are relatively cheap and the crowd is up for it. Special events lure the big-name acts and tend to focus on house and funk DJs, with chilled-out house and retro beats on Thursdays and Fridays.

Good God Small Club *(left)*
53-55 Liverpool Street, CBD
Tel: 02 9267 3787
www.goodgodgoodgod.com
Open: 5pm (8pm Sat)–5am (1am Weds, 2am Thurs) Weds–Sat

This supper club and self-dubbed 'danceteria' is set in an attractive old Spanish quarter restaurant with Flintstone-style faux rock walls, plants hanging from the ceiling and regular club nights. It's the sort of place where there's always something on, from DJs and live bands to music documentary screenings and even trivia – a particularly memorable one picked punter's brains about The Wire television series. Most nights are usually free but occasionally there's a small cover charge – best check the website for current de-

tails. It's a lively place with cheery staff, a no-attitude crowd and a cranking sound system, plus there are booths; hewn from faux plaster-white rock, they make an ideal perch to settle in and let the night unfold. Drinks-wise, the menu includes jugs of Mint Julep and carafes of the club's potent white wine sangria.

Home *(right)*
101 Wheat Road, Darling Harbour
Tel: 02 9266 0600
www.homesydney.com
Open: 10pm–late Fri & Sat

Sister club to the now defunct Home in London, this sprawling mega-club has everything the clubber could desire; a state-of-the-art soundsystem, trippy lasers, world-class big-name DJs flown

in on a regular basis and even water views over Sydney's rather tacky tourist hotspot Darling Harbour from the al fresco roof terrace. It's impressive and futuristic, and although the unisex toilets aren't what you'd call pleasant, it's a rollicking night out and the highly-charged main dance floor transforms into a sea of swaying (and occasionally gurning) clubbers during the Friday night Sublime parties. Running for more than a decade, Sublime is one of the city's best-known club nights, presided over by slashie audio producer, remixer, songwriter KCB and DJ Pee-wee Ferris. If you like your clubbing a tad more intimate, get your freak on in the upstairs bar, which has a smaller area and DJ rocking out the tunes to an equally packed dancefloor. When it all becomes too intense, nothing can beat the terrace bar; it's an excellent spot to gulp some fresh air, let the sweat dry, gab to your friends, or make some new ones. A great club, though Sydney's (fun) police are always sniffing about, and the door policy is tough.

Ivy (top)
330 George Street, CBD
Tel: 02 9240 3000
www.merivale.com
Open: 11am–late Mon–Sat

A playground for the ultra-glamorous, Ivy is Sydney's ultimate den of debauchery. The multi-levelled ode to drinking and mischief begins in the downstairs main bar, which opens up to a huge courtyard with white marbled bars and a Japanese maple tree. Upstairs there are more bars (some require getting past additional clipboard-toting staff) and even an artificial grassed area complete with outdoor showers where poseur clubbers can amp up the naughtiness. The weekly Pure Ivy night attracts Sydney's elite social set, with the city's better-known DJs titillating the crowds – which can number up to hundreds on busy nights. The venue can fit up to 1,000, meaning it's also inadvertently one of the city's most promising pick-up joints. Word has it that the downstairs area is the best place to make friends – but they may not be long-lasting ones. After circling prey downstairs, try your luck upstairs on level five, home to Ivy's infamous Miami-style bar, complete with a swimming pool and cabanas, but don't count on making it past the door unless you've scrubbed up for the occasion.

Kit & Kaboodle (left)
33-37 Darlinghurst Road,
Kings Cross
Tel: 02 9368 0300
www.kitkaboodle.com.au
Open: 8pm–5am Thurs–Sun

With club nights like Kitty Kitty Bang Gang and impishly-named cocktails like Kit Tickler, Kit & Kaboodle is kooky, carefree and always a stack of fun. The good times are spread out inside a two-levelled building just above the Sugarmill pub, and inside it's a wacky world of bordello-style Victorian chairs, plush carpets, antique statues of dragons and party animal clubbers getting sweaty to DJs, such as The Gameboys who play a classic repertoire of house beats. The seating and dance area seem to mesh as one with sassy young music-lovers and armchairs clustered around the DJ, but there's plenty of space for one and all. If you burn off too many calories on the dance floor, you can replenish with pizza and sharing plates, served until 4am. The place fits around 500, so the odds of meeting a special someone increase significantly, too.

Melt (right)
12 Kellet Street, Kings Cross.
Tel: 02 9380 6060
www.meltbar.com.au
Open: 9pm–5am Thurs–Sat

Its location off the main Kings Cross drag means club-cum-live music venue Melt is slightly protected against the passing flotsam and jetsam, but it's still got an element of grunge about it. The main bar has a stage that hosts jazz duos, hip-hop nights, the occasional

party...

duos, hip-hop nights, the occasional album launch, pop groups, seventies disco nights – you name it. It has a loungey vibe with thrift-store chic leather sofas and plump Chesterfields, Art Deco lamps and kooky paintings. In some areas the stripped-back walls are covered with murals and some helpful advice from a previous tenant, who scrawled explicit instructions advising against gambling, drinking and bad language. There's also a mezzanine level with an al fresco balcony for smokers. One of Sydney's friendliest clubs, and one for the musos.

Sapphire Lounge (top)
2 Kellet Street, Kings Cross
Tel: 02 9331 0058
www.sapphirelounge.com.au
Open: 10pm–late Thurs–Sun

So hip it hurts… your wallet. This is a slick hotspot with an achingly cool interior designed by New Yorker Kirk Lenard, who has also whipped up boutiques for Louis Vuitton and Chanel. Set over one level, it's a small club but the interiors glitter as expensively as its moniker – and the crowd isn't bad looking, either, from skinny models to actors and Australian sportsmen. With sexy house tunes, 80s funk and R&B playing most nights, it's the sort of club that likes to amp up the party atmosphere to a maximum crescendo; think samba dancers in full costume, bongo and saxophone players. There's plenty of grooving room near the bar, but hedge-funders and Kings Cross heavyweights prefer to book out the private booths, guzzling expensive Champagne like Louis Roederer Cristal Rose 2000

while mere mortals make do with mixed drinks and cocktails (try the El Managro – aged tequila with Aperol and grapefruit with a hint of Crème de Cacao). The prices can seem steep, but the club often promotes AU$5 cocktails and entry is free before 10pm – so get in early if you want to save some pennies.

Slide (bottom)
41 Oxford Street, Darlinghurst
Tel: 02 8915 1899
www.slide.com.au
Open: 6pm–3am Weds–Sun

Cabaret, burlesque, theatre and drag; if the all-singing, all-dancing Slide came in human form she would be Liza Minelli. Once a former bank, this sophisticated, gay-friendly club occupies two levels of an Art Deco building and its luxe interiors and brilliantly up-lit pink-and-white chequered stage set the scene for a memorable dinner and show. There's seating scattered about the open-level interior with plenty of space to shimmy around to house DJs and live performances on the lower level, and an elegant cocktail lounge upstairs strewn with lots of low leather banquettes for intimate conversations. Keep an eye out for Slide's own productions like El Circo, a fearless and flexible troupe of circus acts, from magician and fire breathers to aerialists, acrobatic artists and live singers. It's all paired with a nine-course French degustation menu – Liza wouldn't have it any other way.

The Tunnel *(top)*
1 Earl Place, Potts Point
Tel: 02 8065 8937
www.tunnelnightclub.com.au
Open: 10pm–late Fri & Sat

After a recent glamorous refurb, The Tunnel is one of the busiest clubs in the Cross area, with a notoriously long queue of sassy women wearing tiny miniskirts and towering stilettos flirting with freshly-shaven men in collared shirts. If you make it past the militant doormen, you're guaranteed a frolicsome time because beyond the exclusivity and overpriced hooch, the dance floor is always packed and everyone seems rearing to get shimmying under the ceiling of dozens of spinning mirror balls. The Tunnel's DJs seem to have an innate sense of knowing exactly when to churn it up, too – expect a mix of up-for-it house and club tracks. To avoid any disappointment or vein-exploding encounters with the doormen, try reserving ahead for priority entry. Or, if you're in a group, there are five private booth areas that can comfortably hold 10 or more clubbers – with packages starting at around AU$350, which includes exclusive entry for your guests, a AU$100 bar tab and two bottles of Champagne. Not a bad entrée to the evening.

World Bar *(left)*
24 Bayswater Road, Kings Cross
Tel: 02 9357 7700
www.theworldbar.com
Open: daily, 1pm–2am (4am Tues / Thurs, 6am Fri–Sun)

This four-storey Victorian terrace is sandwiched between the club and bar mosh-pit of Bayswater Road, Kings Cross, which is one of the busiest parts of Sydney's red light and clubbing districts. The Wham parties on Fridays are the highlight, with house and dance tracks spun by DJs. There's also a generous nod to indie-pop and alternative with various bands scheduled regularly in the cranking back room. Hang outside on the terrace or venture inside, where wildly-wallpapered rooms get crowded on the weekends. The crowd is a mixed bunch but the higher-than-usual backpacker contingent means there's a friendly vibe and drinks are on the cheaper side – which is a welcome respite from criminally expensive cocktails at neighbouring bars and clubs.

LIVE MUSIC

505 *(right)*
280 Cleveland Street, Surry Hills
www.venue505.com
Open: All gigs start at 8:30pm;
Doors open 7:30pm; Mon-Wed
AU$10, Thur-Sat AU$15 / 10
(unless advertised otherwise)

Back in 2004, Kerri Glasscock and Cameron Undy started 505 for the simple reason of creating a local space for the community of inner-city artists / musicians / performers to converge, chat and perform. The idea exploded and at its new, larger venue, 505 has emerged to become one of Sydney's best grass roots live music spaces. From jazz, roots 'n' reggae to Thursday's Sounds of the World program featur-

ing Brazilian, Afro-Cuban, Mambo, Cha Cha Cha, Salsa, Gypsy and folk styles, 505 is the muso's choice, frequented by industry types and in-the-know music-lovers. It doesn't take bookings and the place does get crammed so arrive early if you want to snare a spot to sit. Menus change seasonally, but prices are very reasonable – you'll pay no more than AU$15 for a meal; anything from a goat's cheese and onion tart to a spicy chickpea, spinach and pumpkin salad.

a crooner in a dingy, smoky bar with nothing but shelled peanuts to snack on are long gone – these days they have been replaced by surprisingly decent nibbles, from sharing plates to Italian gourmet pizzas. Sit back and soak it up – it's intimate and there's a real sense of history about the place, which is staffed by some truly passionate music-lovers. Call ahead to find out the schedule of cabaret, jazz and blues performances, order a whisky and get toe-tapping.

 Bar Me
154 Brougham Street (Corner of William Street), Kings Cross
Tel: 02 9368 0894
www.myspace.com/elroccoatbarme
Open: daily, 5pm–midnight
Mon–Fri, 6pm–1am Sat–Sun

It's Australia's oldest jazz club and its hallowed ground, according to Australian musicians. In the 1950s, 60s and right through to the 80s this tiny cellar bar was frequented by all sorts of jazz luminaries – even Frank Sinatra and Sarah Vaughn. The days of listening to

The Basement *(left)*
7 Macquarie Place, Circular Quay
Tel: 02 9251 2797
www.thebasement.com.au.
Open: Mostly every night

The Basement is an icon in the music scene and Sydney's beating jazz heart, hosting all the greats like Dizzie Gillespie and Herbie Hancock, and more eclectic modern acts and international DJs like German duo Jazzanova and scruffy-haired British singer Jamie Cullum. Because it's fairly intimate, it's best not to risk simply showing up and

expecting to waltz on in – dinner-and-show packages sell out very quickly if it's a big name act, as do standing-only tickets. If you're here for a dinner and show, it's generally a two-course meal, but propping oneself up at the bar suits most punters just fine, thank you very much. There are two inside the club; the Blue Note and The Green Room, sturdy wooden bar areas with stools surrounded by walls plastered with old flyers and gig posters. It's especially buzzy during happy hour when schooners will set you back a paltry AU$4 (between Mon–Fri 4.30–6.30pm).

....

Enmore Theatre
118-132 Enmore Road, Newtown
Tel: 02 9550 3666
www.enmoretheatre.com.au
Check Website for schedule

This grand old dame was built in 1908 and opened as a theatre in 1912, but now hosts everything from rock bands and DJs to international comedy acts and orchestra. It's one of Sydney's best spots to see live music and the space is well suited to most styles,

from the acoustic strumming of Jack Johnson, rapping and on-stage antics of Mos Def, to the hip-shaking 1960s funk and soul of Sharon Jones and the Dap Kings. The sprawling interior has a great layout for watching live music – the creaky, carpeted floor on the lower level features removable seats for concerts, and it slopes back so you can always see the stage. Upstairs has fixed, theatre-style seating. There's plenty of room even when an event is a sell-out, but best load up on drinks at the bar because queues can be maddening. The bars are always packed, though it's a canned beer, sprits-in-plastic-cups or pre-mixed ready-to-drink cans situation, to keep us all safe and sound. If you're early and need a feed, there are plenty of cheapie Turkish and Greek restaurants along Enmore Road.

....

The Vanguard   *(right)*
42 King Street, Newtown
Tel: 02 9550 3666
www.thevanguard.com.au
Open: daily, 7pm–midnight
(1am Thurs–Sat)

In the heartland of eclectic Newtown amid a vast array of ethnic eateries and second-hand stores lies the Vanguard. This elegant venue is an old Sydney favourite and tends to host funk, jazz and blues gigs in an intimate dinner-and-show environment. Taking its cue from the 1920s jazz scene, the Van, as it is otherwise known, has poppy red-coloured wallpaper, an ebony staircase leading upstairs and a raised stage that has welcomed a bevy of luminaries like Hawksley Workman and Australia's finest jazz trumpeter James Morrison. The tables for the dinner are all towards the front of the stage area and on the upper mezzanine level, but no matter where you sit you'll always hear a flawless sound thanks to the Cobra Line Array sound system.

ADULT VENUES

Bada Bing
70 Darlinghurst Road, Kings Cross
Tel: 02 9356 2442
www.badabingnightspot.com.au
Open: daily, 8pm–late

As classy and upmarket as they come, Bada Bing is the sort of place that attracts well-behaved stag nights and groups of females, with sexy, sassy surroundings, glittering beaded curtains and plush furnishings. It's a friendly and non-threatening atmosphere (even for the striptease virgin) and the club likes to have fun and create a party atmosphere with hip-hop singers, DJs and special events. If it's a special bash, Bada Bing caters well to private functions and puts on the aptly-named

Thugs & Hoes party where you and your guests can dress up and role play – plus there's a pole stage that can be curtained off for a private show, should you want some extra privacy with the girl of your choice.

Minx
72 Pitt Street, Sydney
Tel: 1300 789 798
www.minxbar.com
Open: 6pm (4pm Fri)–2am Tues–Fri.
Available for lunch bookings and private functions on weekends.

Female-friendly and super-classy, this striptease club is on the nicer side of naughty. It's in the middle of the business district so tends to attract well-heeled financiers and gents, instead of leery louts. Inside, it smacks of class and feels more akin to a gentlemen's smoking lounge, with artwork on the walls and stately Chesterfield armchairs spread over one level, with the strip stage towards the end. The ladies offer sensual private lap dances, and food and cocktails are a big focus, too – after all, getting hot under the collar works up an appetite. Setting it apart from other venues, Minx also caters to women, offering dinner packages and performances featuring a bevy of buff male dancers. It's also probably the only place in Sydney where you can tuck into a sirloin and have a lunchtime lap dance – only on Fridays, though.

Porky's Nite Spot
77 Darlinghurst Road, Kings Cross
Tel: 02 9357 1180
Open: daily, 8pm–late

Porky's is part and parcel of the seedy side of Kings Cross and is famous for being one of those classic sleazy neon-lit titty joints – the kind with burly bouncers and hustlers out the front, and wide-eyed tourists stopping outside to take photographs, hoping to catch a glimpse of jiggery-pokery. The notoriety behind its name means the clientele and the girls aren't as top-notch as a discerning gent might pre-fer, though the shows are entertaining and you should have got the hint by the neon lights flashing promises of live shows and 'girls, girls, girls'. Good for a stag party but keep those sticky paws to yourself – or be thrown out on your arse by one of those burly bouncers.

Showgirls
41 Darlinghurst Road, Kings Cross
Tel: 02 9331 0690
www.worldfamousshowgirls.com.au
Open: daily, 8pm–6am

They say every seat is a front-row seat at Showgirls, because at any one time there are between three and six girls writhing around seductively on stage, which is a whole lot of visual stimula-tion at once. This is the sort of place where the customer is fawned over the minute they arrive, with hostesses wearing tiny white midriff tops pan-dering to your every whim and ensur-ing your glass is never empty. There are a couple of private rooms that seat up to 12 – try one of the double shows, where you can pick two of your favourite girls for a twice-as-nice per-formance. It should be a no-brainer but the club points out that 'your generosity reaps rewards', so tip big and expect to be fussed over. Take a look at the web-site to check out the girls before you go.

CASINOS

Star City
80 Pyrmont Street, Pyrmont
Tel: 02 9777 9000
www.starcity.com.au
Open: 24-hours daily

An easy stroll from central Sydney, there's really only one place to go if you want to burn some cash on rou-lette, baccarat or blackjack, and that's Star City – Sydney's answer to Las Vegas. This sparkling casino hotel has it all – 1,500 slot machines, 200 gam-ing tables, a sprawling sports betting lounge and Trophies Sports bar, the-atres, spas, restaurants and exclusive private rooms like the Baccarat Room with a dedicated buy-in desk and 18 custom-made tables and chairs, or the invitation-only Sovereign Room, where high-rollers – often visiting from Asia – blow squillions without flinching. It's already a perfect mix of glamour and tackiness, though new bosses are plan-ning a AU$640-million overhaul due for completion sometime in 2011. The new goodies will include a new-fangled five-star hotel, a significant boost in the number of gaming tables from 210 to 330 and 'multi-terminal' gaming ma-chines from 59 to 357.

culture...

You may have heard the mutterings about Australia's lack of culture. Perhaps it's because of the lack of national dress (do flip-flops count?), the absence of a national dish or food – apart from a certain yeasty substance we smear on toast – or the embarrassing fact that very few of us know the second verse of our national anthem, the writer of this guide included. Spend some time in Sydney, however, and it will quickly dawn on you that much of our culture is intangible. The best examples are found simply by living la vida local. That means heading to Bondi Beach for a swim, surf or a soft-sand run in the morning, and charring meat in the time-honoured tradition that is the barbecue in the afternoon. You'll also absorb our culture downing a beer or two at an outdoor pub, playing an impromptu game of cricket or frisbee in a park, or while exploring neighbourhoods that are an intrinsic part of the city's multicultural heritage – like Chinatown, the Italian quarter of Leichhardt, or any one of the beachside suburbs from Cronulla in the south right up to Palm Beach in the north.

Absorbing culture is one thing, but there has always been an artistic force at play in Sydney, and the government is beginning to realise the worth of nurturing the industry, funnelling millions of dollars into mammoth projects. This includes a AU$26-million grant to extend the north wing of the Museum of Contemporary Art and plans to re-develop the historic Pier 2/3 at Walsh Bay into a dedicated art space for Australian and international artists, arts companies and performing arts venues. Running the length of Hickson Road, this burgeoning cultural and arts precinct is Australia's version of the West End – home to the Sydney Dance Company and the Sydney Theatre (which is overseen by co-artistic director and Oscar-winning actress Cate Blanchett) and the annual Biennale of Sydney and the Sydney Writer's Festival, among others. It's already an exciting part of the city, but the overall vision is to create a 'cultural ribbon' that stretches from Walsh Bay, right along the foreshore to the iconic Sydney Opera House, a cultural powerhouse on its own, with its concert halls and smaller theatres.

For the razzle-dazzle of musical theatre, we've listed most of the major venues where you can see large-scale productions like Jersey Boys, Cats or Mamma Mia. For visual art, head to the Brett Whiteley Studio or the Tim Olsen Gallery for a taste of great Aussie talent, or the Art Gallery of NSW and Kate Owen Gallery for an insight into the creativity of Australia's indigenous people.

Sydneysiders, however, are losing their taste for big-money galleries. These days, there's a movement towards not-for-profit, artist-run initiatives. By all means head to the Art Gallery of NSW to ogle at priceless Picassos and Monets, and don't miss out on the Museum of Contemporary Art for international exhibits from the big names such as Annie Leibovitz. But to really get a feel for Sydney's diversity and underground creative energy, and to appreciate artistic works often excluded from the commercial realm, take some time to explore the city's edgy, independent galleries, which are sprouting up like mushrooms around gritty inner-city suburbs like Waterloo or Surry Hills. Many are operated by artists themselves, providing a platform for lesser-known artists. Firstdraft, Tap Gallery and Chalk Horse are just a few we've listed. For retro, low-brow, pop surrealism, where you can buy affordable take-home pieces – a tiki mug, perhaps – head to Outré Gallery.

The best gallery, however, is Sydney itself. It's the perfect canvas for annual outdoor art festivals like Art and About or the Biennale of Sydney, when the city's parks, laneways and islands are brought to life with contemporary exhibitions and performances. Visiting in October or November? Don't miss Sculpture by the Sea, when thousands walk along the coastal cliffs between Bondi Beach and Tamarama to view the world's largest annual outdoor sculpture show. The show marks the start of the favourite time of year for most locals – summer and the festival season, when the city's art and cultural industry really lets its hair down. Do as Sydneysiders do and pencil in Tropfest (www.tropfest.com), the Sydney Festival (www.sydneyfestival.org.au) and Gay & Lesbian Mardi Gras (www.mardigras.org. au) on your must-do itinerary.

MULTI-PURPOSE

■ **CarriageWorks** *(left)*
*245 Wilson Street, (corner
of Codrington Street), Eveleigh
Tel: 02 8571 9099
www.carriageworks.com.au
Open: 9am–5pm (1pm Sat). Closed
Sundays unless there is an event on.
Evenings one hour prior to performance.*

Built inside the old Eveleigh Rail Yards, an important piece of Australia's industrial history during the 19th-century, CarriageWorks is an impressive, multi-venue centre focused on contemporary art and culture. The cavernous interiors host large-scale events and theatre performances – anything from Shakespeare to the TEDxSydney Forum, contemporary art and design markets Finders Keepers, hip-hop concerts and even unique charity events like Rethreads, a clothing swap festival organised by Oxfam. It also provides gallery space for the arts sector with numerous rotating exhibitions, and has a huge undercover outdoor space which hosts the Eveleigh Farmer's Market each Saturday featuring 70 authentic producer stallholders who bring seasonal fresh produce from all over NSW, from biodynamic and organic foods, artisan cheese or moreish Chinese dumpling stands (www.eveleighmarket.com.au). It's a mammoth space and there's always something to see or do – best to check the website for current exhibition and performance details.

....

■ **Oxford Art Factory** *(middle)*
*8-46 Oxford Street, Darlinghurst
Tel: 02 9332 3711
www.oxfordartfactory.com
Open: 8pm–6am Weds–Sun*

Taking its cue from Andy Warhol's 1960s Factory, the Oxford Art Factory is a gritty, warehouse-style venue that

has evolved into of the most versatile multi-performance spaces in Sydney. The two-levelled interior features stripped-back Warholian-style murals by local street artists like Beast Man and Numskull and plenty of performance space. Keep an eye on the website for details of the OAF's rotating agenda of edgy installations, exhibitions featuring emerging street scrawlers and established artists and even talks from hip authors such as Bret Easton Ellis. Depending on how long you can put up with the bored, dishevelled-haired too-cool-for-school crowd, it's also an excellent spot to sink a longneck beer or cheap cocktail in the Art After Dark Bar, and a particularly good spot to see live music – past music gigs have included Blackalicious and Eliza Doolittle. The OAF runs a market held on the first Saturday of every month, providing a platform for Sydney's established and emerging artists.

Sydney Opera House *(right)*
Bennelong Point, Sydney
Harbour foreshore
Tel: 02 9250 7111
www.sydneyoperahouse.com
Open: check website for details

It goes without saying that Jørn Utzon's sail-shaped structure is one of the most famous buildings in the world – if not one of the 20th-century's greatest buildings, but despite the name there's a whole lot more going on aside from swooning sopranos. There are seven venues in total, from the opulent concert hall and 1,507-seat Opera Theatre to the Drama theatre, the 398-seat Playhouse theatre and the Studio theatre. It's not just opera and ballet, however; there's something to suit everyone's tastes, from contemporary music gigs, classy big-band acts, comedy and cabaret – and various itineraries to help plan your visit listed on the exhaustive website. The Opera House

culture...

219

deals with more than seven million visitors every year, so we won't add to it other than to advise having a cocktail at the outdoor harbour-view Opera Bar (see Drink) and an unforgettable dinner at Guillaume at Bennelong (see Eat). Even if you don't manage to see a performance, at least walk around the foreshore and admire the thing. It's one of the most recognisable and photographed structures for a reason, covered by around one-million white tiles. It's pretty bloody amazing, is what a Sydneysider would say.

MUSEUMS

 Australian Museum *(left)*
6 College Street, CBD
Tel: 02 9320 6000
www.australianmuseum.net.au
Open: daily, 9.30am–5pm

If you love natural history and dinosaurs, or simply want to terrorise your partner with the sight of a Goliath Tarantula (a South American spider that can grow as large as a dinner plate), the Australian Museum is definitely worth a visit. But it's not just fossils and specimens – this heritage sandstone building also hosts the stunning annual Wildlife Photographer of the Year exhibitions, where you can ogle at photographic masterpieces and engage in workshops to demystify all those buttons on your SLR. It's almost too easy to wander in and have a poke around – it's located right opposite Hyde Park in the centre of Sydney. What's more, the museum recently introduced super-special behind-the-scenes tours, which cost upwards of AU$130 per adult. With only

one per cent of the museum's contents on display, these personal tours offer a peek into the wings that hold the rest of the incredible treasures that are usually reserved for staff and researchers.

DANCE

Bangarra *(bottom)*
Dance Theatre
Pier 4, 5 Hickson Road, Walsh Bay
Tel: 02 9251 5333
www.bangarra.com.au
Open: check website for schedule

Powerful, spellbinding and raw, Australia's first and finest Aboriginal dance company Bangarra has thrived under the artistic direction of Stephen Page, who has led the theatre of 14 dancers since 1991. Seeing one of their productions is an insight and a journey in every sense of the word into the core of Australian indigenous heritage and culture. Each year, the dance theatre performs to 50,000 people around Australia and the world, fusing Aboriginal and Torres Strait Islander traditions and storytelling into explosive, haunting productions such as the critically-acclaimed Bush and Clan, made even more enchanting with the musical creativity of award-winning David Page. The theatre is set at the historic former wharf at Walsh Bay, though the company also performs at the Sydney Opera House.

 Sydney Dance *(right)*
Company
Pier 4, Hickson Road, Walsh Bay
Tel: 02 9221 4811

culture…

A contemporary dance collective, the SDC has been wowing Australians and global audiences for a few decades with explosively creative, dynamic, highly physical, and, at times, raunchy performances drummed up by superstar Spanish-born dancer, choreographer and artistic director Rafael Bonachela. The company performs all around Australia, but in Sydney performances usually show at the Opera House and the Sydney Theatre across the road from its headquarters in Walsh Bay. If you're lucky, you could catch a free show on stage for Festival Inside Out chapter of the annual Sydney Festival. If you want to learn some ballet, hip-hop, funk or simply wiggle your spirit fingers in a jazz class, the SDC dance lessons cost a mere AU$18 and run every day – check the website for timetables.

THEATRES

 Belvoir Street Theatre *(left)*
25 Belvoir Street, Surry Hills
Tel: 02 9699 3444
www.belvoir.com.au
Open: check website for schedule

With its bohemian-chic, eccentric clientele and warm, inviting atmosphere, the Belvoir Street Theatre is one of Sydney's most-loved theatres, formed when 600 members of the theatre-loving community sprang into action in 1984 to prevent the former Nimrod Theatre from demolition. Since it was reborn as the Belvoir, the stage has been graced by all notable Australian luminaries, including Geoffrey Rush, Cate Blanchett and Susie Porter, along with a host of up-and-coming talents. Plays include a vast array of international and local productions, including Hamlet, Waiting for Godot, Summer of

the Seventeenth Doll and Who's Afraid of Virginia Woolf?. The Downstairs Theatre is also home to B Sharp, which presents an annual season of small-scale works, curated by the Belvoir.

Capitol Theatre *(right)*
13 Campbell Street, Haymarket
Tel: 02 9320 5000
www.capitoltheatre.com.au
Open: check website for schedule

The Capitol Theatre is a wonderful example of the glamour associated with going to the theatre in the 1930s – a glance around will immediately conjure up theatregoing Sydneysiders trussed up in their feather boa finery. It has entertained audiences since 1928, and underwent a chrysalis-to-butterfly AU$30-million dollar overhaul in the 1990s, relaunching with much fanfare; newly-spruced and able to accommodate a 110-musician orchestra and 2000-strong audience, the refurb made it a top-notch choice for seeing Guys & Dolls or Fame, stand-up comedy and even concerts – past shows have included Kylie Minogue and Shirley Bassey. The location can't be beaten, either – it's in the heart of Chinatown with plenty of dumpling and BBQ pork joints around for a thrifty dinner-and-show. The theatre has a fascinating history – even if you can't make it to a production, it's worthwhile joining one of the tours, which will explain its history, the architectural elements of John Eberson's theatrical design vision and an inside peek into what it takes to launch a world-class musical production.

Lyric Theatre
80 Pyrmont Street, Pyrmont
Tel: 02 9657 8500
www.starcity.com.au
Open: check website for schedule

culture...

Adjacent to the five-star Star City Casino complex, the Lyric rolls out a busy programme, varying from child-friendly productions like Swan Lake on Ice and the Lion King, music greats like Bob Geldof, Tommy Emmanuel and the Buena Vista Social Club, and the very best of musical theatre. Past productions have included The Phantom of the Opera, Oliver, Mamma Mia!, the world premiere of Doctor Zhivago and Australia's own drag queen extravaganza, Priscilla Queen of the Desert. It seats 2,000 and the well thought-out design means all seats have a line of sight towards the stage – no craning of necks required. It's also a great location, particularly if you feel like a post-show punt at the casino, which boasts a decent selection of restaurants and bars within the complex.

State Theatre *(top)*
49 Market Street, Sydney
Tel: 02 9373 6655
www.statetheatre.com.au
Open: check website for schedule

Preserved by The National Trust of Australia, this gorgeous old 2,000-seat theatre has fabulous acoustics and smacks of old-world glamour, with dress circles, a colossal Koh-I-Noor cut-crystal chandelier (the second largest on earth) and a dramatic, Moulin Rouge-esque scarlet curtain. A fusion of Gothic, Italian and Art Deco design, the sweeping staircase, ballroom and gold domed ceilings are enchanting and put a nudge of romance into a night out at the theatre – you may even be inspired to dust off the elbow-length gloves and smoking jacket. Since the

1930s, the stage of this grand old dame has hosted stars like Cary Grant, Joan Crawford, Bette Midler and Shirley Bassey; these days it hosts musicals, burlesque and even international comedy acts like Arj Barker. Shows are strictly for seated audiences only – which means no moshing.

Sydney Theatre *(bottom)*
22 Hickson Road, Walsh Bay
Tel: 02 9250 1999
www.sydneytheatre.com.au
Open: daily, 9am–8.30pm Mon-Sat;
3–5.30pm Sun

With the luminescent-skinned Cate Blanchett and Andrew Upton as artistic directors, the marvellous Sydney Theatre is Sydney's epicentre for stage magic and the heartland of Australian performing arts. The venue sprawls across the old wharf pier overlooking the harbour west of the Harbour Bridge. It's a modern and impressive space, with an 896-seat auditorium, vaulted ceilings, sweeping foyers and it's green, too – around 70 per cent of the theatre is powered by 1,906 solar panels on the roof. The annual programme features a superb array of theatre from modern productions to Chekhov, Bulgakov and Shakespeare, with a host of local and international production companies including the Sydney Theatre Company, Bell Shakespeare, The Australian Ballet and Abbey Theatre from Ireland. The theatre's vast space also hosts music events, comedy, arts festivals and seminars.

culture...

Theatre Royal
108 King Street, CBD
Tel: 02 9224 8444
www.theatreroyal.net.au
Open: check website for schedule

Plonked right in the heart of the city centre, adjacent to the MLC shopping centre and near various high-end boutiques on King and Castlereagh Streets, the Theatre Royal building was designed by renowned architect Harry Seidler and is an old favourite for dramatic theatre like The Importance of Being Earnest, The Woman in Black and The Hollow Crown. While it's true that many of the large-scale productions were snatched by the multi-million dollar makeover at the Capitol Theatre in Haymarket, the sizeable 1,180-seat auditorium still attracts big-name productions and mega-musicals like Les Miserables, Cats, Rent and Jersey Boys.

GALLERIES

2 Danks Street *(top)*
2 Danks Street, Waterloo
www.2danksstreet.com.au
Open: check website for opening hours as each gallery varies;
Multiple Box is open 24 hours

One gallery? Bah, humbug! How about ten contemporary art galleries? That's what you'll find if you venture south of the city to the edgy, burgeoning arts precinct of Waterloo. The grey-coloured warehouse at 2 Danks Street was a former Kodak factory until Sydney lawyer and philanthropist Leo Christie decided to restore it in a bid to create a flourishing creative community. Today, it's a one-stop shop for art enthusiasts with ten galleries including Annette Larkin Fine Art and Aboriginal and Pacific Art, featuring art from the Tiwi Islands and Arnhem Land in Australia's Northern Territory. Dominik Mersch is a contemporary space that focuses on art from Europe's German speaking culture, while you can pick up limited-edition prints or a bright yellow Andy Warhol bust by Ottmar Hörl at the edgy Multiple Box gallery. Art works up an appetite and Waterloo has some brilliant eateries; in the same warehouse you can stop for lunch at Danks Street Depot, run by slow-food fan chef Jared Ingersoll.

Aquabumps *(bottom)*
151 Curlewis Street, Bondi Beach
Tel: 02 9130 7788
www.aquabumps.com
Open: check website for schedule

Eugene Tan has done Australia a service with his incredible photographer's eye and dedication to capturing the essence of Bondi's beach and surf culture. His stunning photography features images of surfers, along with everyday Bondi scenes of crowded beaches, morning joggers and sunsets. Eugene also shoots from an aerial and underwater perspective – look out for his hauntingly beautiful series of underwater nudes, swimming in the aquamarine depths off Bondi. His blog, a daily documentary shot between the hours of 6am and 7am, is followed by thousands of people from Australia and around the world. If you like what you

culture...

see, head to his Bondi gallery, which sells art-canvas copies of the photographs he takes at the beach every single morning. They can frame any image, though you must give at least two weeks notice.

Art Gallery of New South Wales *(top)*

Art Gallery Road, The Domain
Tel: 02 9225 1700
www.artgallery.nsw.gov.au
Open: daily, 10am–5pm (9pm Weds)

With its façade flanked by elegant Greek columns, the Art Gallery of NSW stands at the foot of The Domain – beautiful parklands only a few minutes away from the city-centre. Check the website for details of touring exhibitions or simply allocate a few hours to explore the gallery's permanent collections, which chronicle world's major arts movements in stunning, light-filled rooms. There are free daily guided tours in various languages along with iPod tours, but it's easy to navigate alone. Among the permanent collections, the Asia wing features towering ceramics, bronzes and even a fully-operating Japanese tearoom, while exquisite paintings from Cezanne, Picasso and Monet are among the Western collection, and the gallery recently paid AU\$5.4-million for Sidney Nolan's First-Class Marksman. Venture downstairs to the fascinating Yiribana Gallery, which displays the world's largest permanent exhibition of Aboriginal Art Torres Strait Islander art, including intricately-painted murals, bark paintings and weavings. If you happen to be in Sydney on a Wednesday night, the gallery remains open until 9pm for Art After Hours, with films, talks, performances, food and wine – a less stuffy, more social way to get an art fix.

At Perry Lane *(middle)*

1 Perry Lane, Rear of 264 Oxford Street, Paddington
Tel: 02 8354 1222
Open: 8am–5pm Fri–Sun (café)

For an art fix washed down with a coffee and a sandwich, wander down to At Perry Lane. This minuscule café is a light-filled oasis away from the sashaying fashionistas shopping up a storm on Oxford Street and a casual way to take in some art over lunch. Spread out over three semi-al fresco levels with a retractable roof and tangles of bougainvillea growing overhead, it's a super-friendly café-slash-gallery on the weekends with an always-interesting rota of emerging artists, live music and tarot readings (by appointment). During the week it's a bit of an all-sorts arts and functions space, hosting fashion launches and boutique PR events.

Australian Centre for Photography *(bottom)*

257 Oxford Street, Paddington
Tel: 02 9332 1455
www.acp.org.au
Open: noon (10am Sat/Sun)–7pm (6pm Sat/Sun). Closed Mondays.

Originally established in 1973 as a meeting place where photographers could exhibit their work, learn the latest tricks of the trade, discuss equipment and network, the ACP has four galleries

sandwiched among the boutiques of Paddington, now widely renowned as the country's longest-running contemporary gallery. If you love photography, want to learn how to make the most of your SLR or want to know more about the passion of (and history of) Australia's best snappers, this is the place to go. Exhibits regularly feature world-class photographers such as Australia's Max Dupain, Bernd and Hilla Becher and Man Ray. Aspiring photographers and admirers should drop in to check out the centre's rotating collection of intriguing exhibits, innovative video workshops and seminars. Admission is free, but many of the seminars and workshops cost money and tickets are only available at the door.

 Brett Whiteley
2 Raper Street, Surry Hills
Tel: 02 9225 1881
www.brettwhiteley.org
Open: 10am–4pm Sat & Sun

Known for his classic Australiana images of the bush and blue waters of Sydney Harbour, Brett Whiteley was one of Australia's most iconic artists. He had a tumultuous life and many of his paintings show his gradual sway to alcohol and drugs, most notably in his droll Self Portrait, painted after he drank three bottles of wine. Sadly, Whiteley's life spun out of control after he became addicted to heroin. He died of an overdose in 1992. However, his prize-winning pieces capture Sydney wonderfully, particularly due to his fondness for using bluish tones, inspired by the harbour. Whiteley lived and worked in this warehouse studio,

which was once an old t-shirt factory, until he died in 1992. Today, the space has been transformed into an art museum managed by the Art Gallery of New South Wales – a tribute to Whiteley's life featuring his completed and unfinished works, furniture, sculptures and memorabilia. The studio is only open during weekends.

 Chalk Horse (top)
94 Cooper Street, Surry Hills
Tel: 02 9211 8999
www.chalkhorse.com.au
Open: noon–6pm Weds–Sat

Blink and you could easily miss Chalk Horse – a hidden contemporary art gallery exhibiting an eclectic array of mostly Australian artists like Tara Marynowsky, whose ethereal watercolours are inspired by Slavic folklore, or Tim Moore, who creates embroidered nudes. Moore is a Brit who actually discovered embroidery on his way from London to Sydney when he forgot his sketch book at the airport and took to using sick bags with the help of in-flight sewing kits! Run by directors fiercely devoted to promoting local artists to international audiences, the gallery also holds events like the global PechaKucha night, where 20 designers or artists in 230 cities around the world show 20 images for 20 seconds, speaking about each image as they go.

 Firstdraft (bottom)
116 Chalmers Street, Surry Hills
Tel: 02 9698 3665
www.firstdraftgallery.com
Open: noon–6pm Weds–Sun

culture...

This non-profit, artist-run studio is managed entirely by volunteers and practising artists. It is one of the pioneers of the boom in artist-run initiatives in Australia, giving big breaks to budding artists since 1986 – many of whom have gone on to do great things, such as exhibiting at the Sydney Biennale or becoming gallery curators themselves. There are three – occasionally four – galleries displaying various exhibitions and Firstdraft also runs an interesting programme of Artist Talks with every exhibition, allowing audiences to learn more about the nuts and bolts behind the art. On the final Sunday of each show at 4pm, the exhibiting artist speaks about their work – it's a great way to get a sense of who they are, understand the intricacies of their creativity and ask questions.

Kate Owen Gallery *(top)*
680 Darling Street, Rozelle
Tel: 02 9555 5283
www.kateowengallery.com
Open: 11am–6pm Weds–Sun
(or by appointment)

If you're keen for a closer look at some of Australia's best Aboriginal artwork, the Kate Owen Gallery should be high on the itinerary. The gallery specialises in contemporary indigenous art, which is spread out over a three-levelled, airy space in Rozelle, a Bohemian suburb over the Anzac Bridge, just a few minutes' drive from the CBD. There are around 800 works by emerging and established Aboriginal artists, who hail from the central and western desert regions, including pieces from the Warlukurlangu Artists' Aboriginal

Corporation in Yuendumu, a community some 300-kilometres northwest of Alice Springs. All works are authenticated, and range from smaller pieces under AU$500 to larger, more complex works. The studio is owned by Kate Owen, a British-born artist who grew up in Australia.

The Museum of *(bottom)* Contemporary Art (MCA)
140 George Street, The Rocks
Tel: 02 9245 2400
www.mca.com.au
Open: daily, 10am–5pm

Surrounded by lawns and facing the busy ferry terminal at Circular Quay, the attractive MCA offers fantastic look-see-sigh potential for the contemporary art-lover. There's always an interesting rota of high-profile, temporary exhibits from Australian and international artists. Led by the marvellous Scotswoman director Elizabeth Ann Macgregor, the MCA has gone from strength to strength over the past few years – she's managed to lure a bold range of sometimes controversial art, from celebrity snapper Annie Leibovitz's naked (and pregnant) Demi Moore to the startling taxidermy horse by Italian l'enfant terrible, Maurizio Cattelan. There's always something to see and talk about, and the views across the harbour to the Opera House from the café aren't half bad, either. Free guided tours run daily at 11am and 1pm and on weekends at 11am, 1pm and 3pm, though time your visit well – the MCA received a whopping multi-million dollar grant from the government in 2010, with extensions to the

MUSEUM OF CONTEMP

north of the building set for completion in 2012.

Outre Gallery *(top)*
Shop 7, 285a Crown Street, Surry Hills
Tel: 02 9332 2776
www.outregallery.com
Open: noon (11am Sat)–7pm (8pm Thurs, 6pm Sat, 4pm Sun). Closed Mon/Tues.

Here's a gallery that gave a middle-finger salute to the high-brow, snooty arts scene. Masters of quirk and cool, Outre is a hipster's dream, started by art-lover Martin McIntosh, and its popularity spreads throughout the country, with galleries in Melbourne and Perth along with Sydney. Be it low-brow, retro or pop surrealism, the two-levelled gallery always has a couple of genuinely friendly staffers floating around happy to answer questions, and has a fresh, ever-changing rota of exhibitions. There are all sorts of cool, eclectic buys – from Polynesian-style tiki mugs which Outre imported from Spanish ceramics company Porcelanas Pavón, to super-cool limited-edition prints, vinyl toys and much, much more.

Tap Gallery
278 Palmer Street, Darlinghurst
Tel: 02 9361 0440
www.tapgallery.org.au
Open: daily, noon–6pm (evenings vary when there is a performance or event)

A self-described 'open-policy, artist-run collective', Tap has numerous exhibition spaces spread across 900-square-metres of space for emerging artists to exhibit and promote their work – it's well-loved by the community and has nurtured the careers of numerous Australian artists like Andrew Logan, Carlos Barrios, Mark Hanham and James Powditch. Tap is also a boon for Sydneysiders who need entertaining; along with exhibitions, the gallery functions as a visual and performing arts centre, and there's an exhaustive number of shows and events, from classes in life drawing, poetry and songwriting, to comedy and short film screenings on the 'Caught Short' evenings. There's also a second-hand book library where you can pick up a well-thumbed novel, and a quirky-cool organic café in which to grab a bite.

Tim Olsen Gallery *(bottom)*
63 Jersey Road, Woollahra
Tel: 02 9327 3922
www.timolsengallery.com
Open: daily, 10am (noon Sun)–6pm (5pm Sat/Sun)

One of Sydney's most esteemed galleries, Tim Olsen's features the landscape art work of his father, the beret-wearing John Olsen, who is one of Australia's most renowned artists and who remarkably continues to paint every day, even in his 80s. As well as Olsen's works, the gallery exhibits the work of a stable of other emerging contemporary artists like Rex Dupain, Martine Emdur and Fiona Greenhill. Its popularity and expansion since 1993 saw the move to new premises on Jersey Road in the upmarket suburb of Woollahra, into a white mansion, which has much more room for exhibits and is spread out over two levels. Works by overseas-based artists are also exhibited in a bid to promote a dialogue between Australian art and its international contemporaries.

White Rabbit *(opposite)*
30 Balfour Street, Chippendale
Tel: 02 8399 2867
www.whiterabbitcollection.org
Open: 10am–6pm Thurs–Sun

Part-gallery, part-teahouse, the White Rabbit houses an astonishing amount of contemporary Chinese art – thought to be the world's largest and most significant collection. Owned by husband-and-wife founders Kerr and Judith Neilson, the gallery came about when Judith's tutor introduced her to a burgeoning contemporary art scene exploding in China. Judith began to collect her own pieces and it grew from there. Set in the gritty heart of Chippendale's urban streets, the space spans four floors of a former knitting factory, with airy exhibition spaces, a library of catalogues, artist biographies and surveys of Chinese contemporary art, and a gorgeous teahouse where in-house Uighur tea expert Yusuf serves up an impressive range of Chinese-grown herbal teas. It's a fascinating insight into the minds of gifted Chinese artists, who are often forced to go underground to pursue their passion, especially due to a spate of crackdowns by Chinese authorities. There's plenty to learn – if you want to know more, passionate tour leaders explain all the details on guided tours each Thursday to Sunday at 11am and 2pm.

culture...

shop…

Whether you're in need of a Swarovski crystal-studded evening gown or a snazzy pair of Lacoste sneakers, Sydney's shopping is getting better and bigger and so are our home-grown designers. Collette Dinnigan, Alex Perry, Akira Isogawa, Sass & Bide and Alice McCall have seduced even the most critical fashionistas on international catwalks, and there are scores of other hot-to-trot emerging designers to snap up before they become big. Where to flex your Amex? With the majority of the city's shopping malls, department stores and arcades – including the gleaming, behemoth new city Westfield – literally within a few blocks of each other, it's all too easy to spend hours shopping in the CBD. Westfield truly does trump them all, but we've listed all the best ones including the triple-domed Queen Victoria Building, which was described by Pierre Cardin as the most beautiful shopping centre in the world.

For big-name luxury brands, slap on a wide-brimmed hat and some Prada sunglasses à la Julia in Pretty Woman when you totter down the city's Castlereagh Street, which is the closest thing Sydney has to New Bond Street or Fifth Avenue. Here you will find all your Jimmy Choos, Louis Vs and Chanels lined side by side along with frighteningly expensive sparkles from Tiffany & Co., Bvlgari and Australian jewellers Canturi and Cerrone.

For those miserably sans Black Amex, wander along Crown Street in Surry Hills to fossick for a vintage find – it's where a clutch of second-hand stores sell superbly-maintained pieces from the 50s, 60s and 70s, from quilted Chanel handbags to retro Dior sunglasses. The long, winding King Street in Newtown is Sydney's other second-hand Mecca. Stylish men will want to check out the man-friendly boutiques along Burton Street in Darlinghurst, while women will swoon over the latest styles in the boutiques of Paddington, Darlinghurst, Surry Hills and Woollahra.

The edgiest, most fashion-forward boutiques are conveniently concentrated around Oxford Street, renowned as the best shopping strip in Sydney. It's a long one, so wear flat shoes – you've been warned. For more devastatingly hip boutiques, veer off Oxford Street at William Street, and then again at Glenmore Road, what fashionistas affectionately call 'The Intersection'.

What else to buy? The balmy summers mean Sydneysiders are particularly skilled at pulling together an effortless summer, beach-to-bar look. If you like what the Bondi hipsters are wearing, you can pinch their style by shopping at the boutiques along Gould Street, only a street back from the sand. Australian swimwear is renowned around the world, too – so be sure to look out for our top bikini designers Zimmermann and Tigerlily.

Lastly, do as the fashion editors do and spend half a day browsing around Sydney's outdoor markets. They're usually held on weekends and you're nearly guaranteed to find something offbeat and utterly unique. Again, we've listed them all here. Now, go forth and shop, you style maven.

CENTRAL BUSINESS DISTRICT (CBD)

▣ CASTLEREAGH STREET

Canturi (80) One of Australia's best-known jewellers has a dazzling array of sparkles snapped up by Nicole Kidman, Oprah Winfrey and Kylie Minogue.

Cerrone (77) Popping the question? Nic Cerrone's engagement rings are loved by stars and Sydney's most stylish society couples.

Chanel (70) The flagship Sydney store stocks all the latest from Chanel – including those iconic quilted handbags, sunglasses and elegant perfumes.

Jimmy Choo (41) For SATC sexiness, snap up a pair of snakeskin stilettos with a clutch to match.

Louis Vuitton (63) Browse through LV's carefully displayed monogrammed luxurious leathergoods and luggage synonymous with this mega-brand.

Prada (15) Top-of-the-range buttery soft hobo bags and premium sunglasses in classic Italian styles.

▣ AROUND CBD

Apple *Corner of George & King Streets*
Go on – do it. Ditch that dull-as-dishwater PC and become a sexy Mac person. Find the latest and the greatest Macbooks, iPods and iPads in this glossy, three-levelled temple of electronica, plus all the accessories and a suitably hipster crowd.

Paspaley Pearls *2 Martin Place*
Founded in 1952, Paspaley sells exquisite jewellery featuring luminescent West Australian pearls.

▣ CBD MALLS & DEPARTMENT STORES

David Jones
Corner of Market & Castlereagh Streets
An esteemed department store in the vein of Harrods or Saks, with separate buildings devoted to multi-levelled men's and women's fashion, luxury homeware, beauty and fragrances.

The Galeries Victoria
Corner of Park & George Streets
This light, airy, four-levelled shopping centre includes behemoth bookstore Books Kinokunya, Mango and Incu boutique – featuring edgy local and international designers.

MidCity Centre
Pitt Street Mall
Newly-renovated, there are 45 chain store retailers over four levels including elegant basics at Witchery, streetwear at General Pants, stylish menswear at Politix and cute pyjamas at Peter Alexander.

MLC Centre
Corner of King & Castlereagh Streets
Smaller retailers and luxury designer stores including Gucci and Lonchamp.

Myer
Pitt Street Mall
One of Sydney's best-known department stores has a gargantuan cosmetics and fragrances floor and numerous upper levels packed with mid-to high-end Australian designers, global fashion brands, lingerie and shoes.

Queen Victoria Building
Corner of Market & George Streets
This ornate, 19th-century arcade is exquisite with copper domed ceilings, 200 contemporary fashion boutiques and some of Australia's top upmarket chain stores over five levels.

Strand Arcade
Pitt Street Mall
A striking 19th-century Victorian shopping mall with some of Sydney's most covetable fashion boutiques including Lisa Ho, Manning Cartell, Jayson Brunsdon, Little Joe, The Corner Shop and the city's favourite milliner, Strand Hatters.

Westfield City
Pitt Street Mall & Market Streets
An ode to shopping, the new mall has it all – labels include Carla Zampatti, Diane von Furstenberg, DKNY Jeans, Gap, Gucci and top Australian fashion brands Leona Edmiston, Mulberry, Sass & Bide, Tigerlily and Zimmerman. At the time of writing this guide, the soon-to-be-opened boutiques included Bottega Veneta, Calvin Klein, Christian Louboutin, Miu Miu, Prada and the long-awaited flagship Zara store, which will be the first in Australia.

BONDI

Westfield Bondi Junction
500 Oxford Street
A gigantic one-stop shopping mall with more than 400 fashion, homeware and beauty retailers including Louis Vuitton, Sass & Bide, Karen Millen, Polo Ralph Lauren and both Myer and David Jones department stores.

◼ GOULD STREET

From St Xavier (84) Too-cool-for-school fashion for men and women – hipster labels include Religion, Chronicles of Never, Lila and Buddhist Punk.
Grandma Takes A Trip (79) Premier vintage and retro fashion boutique with international pieces from the 50s, 60s and 70s.
Jatali Bright, fun and fresh women's fashion and jewellery by Sydney designer Tali Jatali.
Ksubi (82) Super-hip Australian denim and fashion, from edgy eyewear to distressed leather boots.
One Teaspoon (86) Feminine and fun Australian women's label featuring casual denim, sunglasses and street chic pieces.
Tuchuzy (90) This boutique is loved by Sydney's seriously fashion-forward, stocking both menswear and womenswear, including Sass & Bide, Allanah Hill and Dangerfield.

◼ CURLEWIS STREET

Me and Moo (5/157) Classy, elegant fashion from esteemed labels like Purl Harbour.
Miljo (23c) On-trend Scandinavian design store with stylish jewellery, fashion, and homeware.
Milk Bar 4/157 A boutique filled with lots of edgy Australian labels including Manning Cartell, Woodford & Co, Hussy and Ru Mu.

■ AROUND BONDI

Bikini Island *36 Campbell Parade*
Rack upon er, rack of all the best Australian bikini brands, including Zimmerman, Jets, Seafolly and Tigerlily.
Camilla Beach House *132a Warners Ave* Sydney's kaftan queen Camilla Franks creates flamboyant, multi-coloured kaftans, jumpsuits and slip dresses to take you from beach to bar.

POTTS POINT & ELIZABETH BAY

■ MACLEAY STREET

Arida (61) High-end luxury brands, furniture and homeware like Givenchy, Nina Ricci, Lanvin and Alexander McQueen.
Becker Minty *(Corner Greenknowe Ave)* Co-owners Christopher Becker and Jason Minty travel the world to source unique curios, jewellery and collectables.
Becker Minty Woman *(Corner Greenknowe Ave)* Fabulous women's fashion boutique with a cool selection of gowns and handbags.
Blueprint *(Shop 3, 46a)* Gifts, inspiring household items and lust-worthy coffee table books from brands like U+ from Umbra, Reisenthel and Icon Concepts.
Macleay on Manning *(Shop 1, 85)* Jewellery, coffee table books, ceramics and homeware from Missoni, Sonja Rykiel and Fornasetti.
Mon Petit Chou (115) Eclectic women's fashion from Australian, New Zealand and international brands.

■ AROUND MACLEAY STREET

Bloodorange *35 Elizabeth Bay Road*
Hipper-than-thou boutique for women stocking Terry De Havilland shoes, Australian designer Karla Spetic, A.P.C., Lulu Frost and Daryl K.
Restricted Premises *3 Roslyn Street*
Predominantly menswear with brands including Chronicles Of Never, Eley Kishimoto and Akira.

PADDINGTON

■ WILLIAM STREET

Andrew McDonald (58) This bespoke shoemaker creates quality leather shoes and boots, fine-tuning his traditional cobbling skills in London.
Belinda (29) A womenswear boutique with an array of top-end designers from Marni, Lanvin and Dries Van Noten to niche collections of up-and-coming Australian designers.
Jac + Jack (39) Fluid, stylish men's and women's cashmere, tees and scarves in neutral hues.
Leona Edmiston (88) An Australian designer renowned for her womenswear and accessories – check out her range of clutches, belts and scarves.
Lucette (23) Eclectic boho pieces with an edge – think silk harem pants and embellished blazers.
Rose & Ruby (5) Ethereal dresses made from silk, French lace and tulles
The Corner Shop (43) Features the very best of Australian femme designers like Karla Spetic, Marnie Skillings, Philip Lim and Alexander Wang.

Tigerlily (37) An Australian swimwear label selling everything a stylish Sydney girl needs to hit the beach, from sexy bikinis and kaftans to beach bags.

■ OXFORD STREET

Aesop (72a) Originally from Melbourne, Aesop's sexy body and bath products have a cult following.

Ariel (42) Fantastic selection of books with handwritten recommendations from staff.

Assin (15/T2 Verona Street) Edgy, high-end designs for men and women from Christian Dior to Lanvin.

Berkelouw (19) New fiction and non-fiction bookstore with a fab second-hand section and a jazz café upstairs.

Bianca Spender (9) Daughter of Australian fashion designer Carla Zampatti, Bianca's sharp tailoring and loosely draped pieces flatter the female form as beautifully as her mother's collections.

General Pants (346) Urban men and women's streetwear chain store, for festival-friendly fashion.

Gorman (30) Super-hip utilitarian clothing for women with a feminine edge.

Harlequin Market (94a) This upmarket vintage boutique stocks pre-loved designer fashion and pieces from American jewellery designer Kenneth Jay Lane.

Incu (256) A fashionable boutique that even the Satorialist would approve of – it also stocks Topshop and Topman.

Kiehls (396) The flagship store of this popular New York-based beauty brand stocks all the greats, including the covetable lip balm.

Shag (34) Vintage dresses, fur stoles and quirky second-hand items well worth the fossick.

Style Council (22) A hip den of menswear from Australian and international designers.

■ GLENMORE ROAD (CORNER OF OXFORD ST)

Alannah Hill (118/ 120 Oxford Street) Exquisitely feminine, eclectic pieces with lots of feathers, floral and faux fur.

Bassike (26 Glenmore Road) The name says it all – jersey and Japanese denim basics with an edge and a killer fit.

Camilla and Marc (2-16 Glenmore Road) From chic bikinis to luxe dresses and turbans, anything from this Australian brother-and-sister fashion duo is lust-worthy.

G-Star (130 Oxford Street) An ode to sexy denim and urban clothing for both men and women.

Ginger & Smart (2-16 Glenmore Road) Sydney women adore G&S dresses, with details like edgy laser-cutting and vibrant colours.

Kirrily Johnston (2-16 Glenmore Road) Kirrily's wearable, sexy modern womenswear has caught the eye of Hollywood starlets, with striking striped tribal dresses for women and men's t-shirts, vests and cardigans.

Ksubi (140 Oxford Street) Formerly known as Tsubi, this store's distressed denim, slinky skinny jeans and cool sunglasses are worshipped by Sydney hipsters.

Mecca Cosmetica (126 Oxford Street) An excellent range of global make-up and hair and beauty brands

shop…

from Nars, Chautecaille, Stila and Bumble & Bumble.

Parlour X (213 Glenmore Road) Owner Eva Galambos handpicks designer fashion from around the globe, with labels that include Vivienne Westwood and Zac Posen.

Peep Toe (Shop 4, 2-16 Glenmore Road) A women's shoe emporium with stilettos, wedges and thigh-high boots all artfully displayed in boudoir surrounds.

Sass & Bide (132 Oxford Street) From stovepipe jeans to luxe, embellished dresses and blazers, this Australian design duo is Australia's hottest fashion export.

Scanlan & Theodore (122 Oxford Street) Fashionistas swoon over this Melbourne design house's stunning, high-end designs.

Shakuhachi (168 Oxford) The flagship store of this Aussie designer sells cool, urban womenswear.

Willow (3a Glenmore Road) Whimsical summery dresses and stunning silk lingerie with handcrafted beaded detailing.

Zambesi (5 Glenmore Road) Stylishly tailored, killer-cut women's and menswear in black, black, and yet more black.

Zimmermann (2-16 Glenmore Road) Upmarket Australian design partners Nicky and Simone are the queen of gorgeous swimwear and floaty, feminine dresses.

WOOLLAHRA

◼ QUEEN STREET, WOOLLAHRA

Akira Ishogawa (12a) Minimalism has never been sexier in something designed by Australia's most critically-acclaimed, Kyoto-born fashion designer.

Attic (118) Furniture, fashion and luxury homeware including Missoni, Marc by Marc Jacobs, See by Chloé and more.

Collette Dinnigan (104) As one of Australia's most celebrated fashion designers, Collette Dinnigan's exquisite, delicately-beaded dresses are deservedly loved by Hollywood celebrities.

Orson & Blake (83) Luxurious, modern designs for the home and fashion accessories.

Ruby & Min (128) Clothing and accessories from local and international brands such as Nolita, Velvet and Graham & Spencer.

Quincy (76) Buttery-soft leather handbags from Marc Jacobs, Manolo Blahnik, Christian Lacroix, Diane von Furstenberg and more.

Saba (80) Contemporary and stylish label for men and women with an emphasis on the silhouette.

Tim O'Connor (86) Stylish, slinky, high-end womenswear in luxe fabrics.

Trelise Cooper (82) Feminine 50s-style skirts, and colourful summery prints for the avant-garde femme.

◼ AROUND WOOLLAHRA

Marnie Skillings *123 Edgecliff Road* Marnie's eponymous label is stocked at top-end fashion boutiques – this is her flagship boutique featuring styles in high-calibre fabrics, textures and modern shapes.

SURRY HILLS & DARLINGHURST

▦ SOUTH DOWLING STREET

Alice McCall (319) The new flagship store of this covetable Australian women's fashion designer – her pieces have made waves overseas, catching the eye of Chloe Sevigny and Topshop.

My Boudoir (323) This elegant boudoir sells pre-loved Gucci, Dior and Chanel, among other exclusive brands.

▦ BURTON STREET

Footage (13C) A one-stop footwear shop for hipster men – along with Nike and Adidas, footwear includes Skinny Nelson and Friends, Ernest Sewn, Nathan Smith and Paige Denim.

Lyrix (13A) Well-curated collections for both genders, featuring Japanese labels Preen, Kenzo and Journal Standard.

Supply (20) The fashion-forward man will find stylish street brands here, including Neighbourhood, Supreme, Visvim, Perks and Mini.

One of a Kind (114) Pick up an on-the-pulse tie or chequered shirt with local designers and international labels from Superfine, Dior, Margiela and Comme des Garçons.

▦ BOURKE STREET

The Candy Store (561) You will be the proverbial kid in this boutique, chock-a-block with cutting-edge fashion for women.

Paris Texas (729) Sells a bevy of emerging and established Australian designers for men and women.

▦ CROWN STREET

Flight 001 (285A) Super-cool boutique devoted to travel with trendy earplug cases, must-have patterned eyemasks and awesome luggage from brands like Rimowa.

Grandma Takes A Trip (263) Sells a top-end vintage collection of clothing and accessories - fossick enough and you may walk away with a Chanel handbag or a Dior dress.

Minty Meets Munt (275) Cute, youthful women's fashion label – think lilac skirts, striped tees and fitted dresses.

Via Alley (Shop 3, 285A) Edgy fashion from Japanese brands like Cosmic Wonder, Mercibeaucoup, Ne-Net, Zucca and Tsumori Chisato, homeware, jewellery, art books and magazines.

Wheels & Doll Baby (259) Rockabilly, leopard and lingerie as outerwear just like Katy Perry or Gwen Stefani.

▦ AROUND SURRY HILLS & DARLINGHURST

Division2 *168 Campbell Street* A world of men's street denim with labels like SealKay, Three Over One, Joe Black and Superfine.

shop...

Half Sleeve *Shop 3, 133 Goulburn Street*
Edgy men's street t-shirts with local and international labels like Fred Perry, 10 Deep, Mishka, Nooka and The North Face.

MARKETS

Bondi Markets
Bondi Beach Public School,
Campbell Parade.
Open: 10am–4pm Sundays
Vintage, cool streetwear fashion and jewellery from emerging designers – many who go on to launch successful labels, only footsteps from the sand.

Fringe/ Bar Markets
106 Oxford Street, Paddington.
Open: 10am–4pm Saturdays
Hipster fashion, creative jewellery and designs from fashion college graduates – plus it's on the city's best-known shopping strip.

Glebe Markets
Corner of Derby Place and
Glebe Point Road, Glebe.
Open: 10am–4pm Saturdays
Kooky vintage and craft market, with crates of rock 'n' roll records, bright green velvet blazers, flares and '80s T-shirts.

Kirribilli Markets
Bradfield Park, off South
Alfred Street, Milsons Point
Open: 9am–3pm second
Sunday in the month.

Theses once-monthly markets are a Mecca for vintage, particularly if you're there on a day when a socialite is selling off her unwanted clothes – get there well before the official market time to snatch bargainous luxury cast-offs.

Paddington Markets
395 Oxford St, Paddington.
Open: 10am–4pm Saturdays
Launching the careers of some of Australia's best-known designers including Lisa Ho and Pablo Nevada, these markets are set in the grounds of a church and school. There are 250 stalls selling fashion, jewellery and unique buys.

shop...

play…

Ahhh, Sydney Harbour. It's at the top of the list for every visitor and undeniably one of the most devastatingly beautiful harbours in the world. We'd bet our last Australian dollar that a good chunk of your time will be spent oohing and ahhing at its sheer beauty, so we've listed numerous ways to make the most of it in this chapter.

There's probably no better way to take in the mesmerising blue green waters than aboard a yacht, kayak, ferry or chartered boat cruise, though it's equally as stunning from the shore, particularly when you lace up your walking shoes for a stroll around the tranquil, foreshore harbour reserves, passing sheltered swimming coves, pockets of native bushland and multi-million dollar mansions – many with views of the Opera House and the Harbour Bridge. After you've papped the bridge – or what Australians call 'The Coathanger' – from every angle, you can even slip into a (hideous) grey jumpsuit and climb it on an organised tour for a top-of-the-world aspect over Sydney, and a truly enviable pic to upload to your Facebook profile.

With such a sparkly harbour and kilometres of magnificent beaches, it's little wonder most of the sporting and leisurely pastimes we've listed are outdoorsy pursuits – namely swimming, surfing, yachting, kayaking, golfing and strolling around the coastline, parks and gardens. By all means hit the bars and the clubs at night, but during the day, get outside, soak up the natural beauty and feel the sea breeze on your skin.

Every visitor should, at the very least, do the Bondi to Bronte beach walk, but if your idea of strenuous activity is lugging a tray of gin and tonics back from the bar, make like a celebrity and take a scenic seaplane trip, flying above the harbour and coastline from Rose Bay, before skidding across the water near Palm Beach. Too adventurous for you? Then simply unfurl a beach towel and spend the day horizon-

tal on the sand – suitably smeared with 30+ sunscreen, of course. Australian sun is brutal – you've been warned.

There isn't enough space (or adjectives) to describe Sydney's 100 or so beaches but we've listed a selection of the best, whether you want to pose with fashionable hipsters at Bondi or Tamarama (called Glamourama by locals), learn to surf, scuba dive or snorkel at Manly, or indeed bob around on an inflatable sunlounger at a picturesque harbour beach like Balmoral. Word to the wise – if you do decide to swim at a surf beach, do yourself a favour and stay between the red and yellow surf lifesaving flags, which mark out the safest area to swim. The swells and currents (known as 'rips') can be swift, overpowering and they frequently take even the strongest Australian beachgoer completely by surprise. Put simply, around 100 people die each year at our beaches, so don't be one of them. If you do run into trouble, don't splash around like a maniac, panic or try to swim against the current – instead, raise one hand in the air to catch the attention of lifesavers.

If we've successfully spooked you away from the waves, don't worry. How about a refreshing dip in an ocean pool? Hewn from the saltwater rockpools and craggy cliffs alongside many of Sydney's beaches, most of these outdoor swimming pools are free, though some of the most iconic are maintained and require a small entrance fee. We've listed the best ones, along with some other swimming pools in which to do some al fresco laps.

Lastly, what's a holiday without a massage? Are we right, or are we right? If you're in desperate need of some kneading, scrubbing and pampering, rest assured our hand-picked spas are covered here, whether you want an eyebrow tidy or wax-on-wax-off, an hour-long uplifting botanical massage or even the ultimate hedonistic experience, a 24-carat gold facial.

play...

BEACHES

Eastern Suburbs

Bondi needs no introduction – it's Sydney's most famous beach, perennially abuzz with stylish beachgoers and surfers paddling out to the waves. There's also scores of cafés, bars, restaurants, boutiques and weekly markets – it's little wonder locals who live here refuse to move elsewhere. It's an easy walk along the coastline to Tamarama (aka Glamourama), an equally stylish, though much smaller beach. The walk continues to Bronte and Coogee, both relaxed beaches with parks to the rear for picnickers, beachside cafés and pubs. Further south, Maroubra is widely regarded as the best surf beach in the eastern suburbs.

Harbour Beaches

Facing the north headlands, Balmoral is the harbour's longest and prettiest beach, with sheltered coves, rolling lawns, excellent eateries and activities like sailing, snorkelling and kayaking. Framed by shady parkland, the tiny strip of sand known as Chinamans is a favourite for picnickers – though hidden. The beach and park at Clifton Gardens faces Chowder Bay, with a netted swimming area and a few excellent harbourfront restaurants and cafés. Nearby, Obelisk is one of the city's only beaches where you can legally get an all-over tan. In the Eastern Suburbs, Nielsen Park has a netted swimming area, and is framed by a thick grove of trees, gently sloped lawns and an always-busy café fronting the harbour. A short walk away, the miniscule Milk Beach faces the city skyline. Also in

the Eastern Suburbs, Camp Cove has a netted swimming area, as does Redleaf pool – a portion of harbour and petite strip of sand enclosed by an old wooden wharf, with floating barges to jump off.

Northern Beaches

Manly is one of the North Side's most popular and busiest beaches, and so sizeable it's been divided into various sections; Queenscliff, North Steyne, and South Steyne. There's a plethora of things to do; grab a *gelato* or coffee along the corso, hire a bike and cycle along the promenade, learn to surf, have a dip at the sheltered cove known as Shelley Beach towards the southern end or hire a kayak and paddle to Store Beach, which is only accessible from the water. Head further north for Freshwater, a smaller beach with some excellent restaurants. The best surfing beaches are North Narrabeen, the northern end of Newport, Avalon and Warriewood. Lastly, every Sydney visitor should drive to the end of the Palm Beach peninsula, with its mega-rich mansions, clifftop lighthouse and, if you're lucky, to catch a glimpse of iconic soap opera Home & Away being filmed.

BOAT TRIPS

Captain Cook

No.6 Jetty, Circular Quay
Tel: 02 9206 1111
www.captaincook.com.au
Open: daily, 8.30am–7pm

North Narrabeen Beach

play...

Visitors are usually stunned by the sheer size of Sydney Harbour. There's so much of it to explore and the AU$39 Captain Cook hop-on, hop-off Harbour Explorer makes it all too easy. Board one of the Rocket Ferries, which run at regular intervals between eight drop-off points, like Shark Island, Watson's Bay and Taronga Zoo. The pass is valid for 24-hours so you can take your time exploring each destination.

Majestic Cruises
Tel: 02 8296 7222
www.magisticcruises.com.au

As well as offering the typical tourist lunch and dinner cruises, Majestic has a AU$20 one-hour sightseeing cruise that departs every day from Circular Quay at 3pm. It's perfect if you're pressed for time and still want to glimpse the 'best of' sights, hear some sightseeing commentary and get some snaps to prove that yes, you were actually here.

Sydney Ferries
www.sydneyferries.info

These iconic yellow and green ferries have trundled across the harbour for decades and they're a cheap, convenient and easy way to explore the city, with fares starting at AU$5.60. Some of the best journeys are Circular Quay to Manly (around 30 minutes) or Circular Quay to Watsons Bay. The Zoo Pass is also a good deal; it includes a 12-minute trip from Circular Quay to Taronga Zoo Wharf, entry and a return fare – all for under AU$50.

CYCLING

Bikes are permitted almost anywhere in the city except for the major arterial roads, but be warned – the hilly streets can turn a casual pedal into thigh-burning hell. Take extra care while you're out because Sydney isn't as bike-friendly as its nemesis Melbourne, though the current Lord Mayor is on a mission to change that with new campaigns educating motorists and cycle paths being built across the city. Look for the green bicycle track marked onto roads and keep your skull safe with a helmet – it's the law.

Centennial Parklands Cycle Hire
100m past the intersection of Grand Drive & Hamilton Drive, Centennial Park
Open: daily, 9am–5pm (last hire 4pm)

With its lakes, grassy fields and gardens, this tranquil park is a cyclist's heaven. Grab a rental bike from as little as AU$15 per hour, pedal around on a 3.8-kilometre cycling lane, and finish up with a picnic lunch.

Humble Vintage
Available from Darlinghurst and North Bondi locations.
www.thehumblevintage.com

The concept of renting out lovingly-restored vintage bicycles began in Melbourne, and only recently came to Sydney. Pick up a vintage racer, tuck a quirky Cyclist's Guide to Sydney map in your back pocket and head off to explore the owner's handpicked city sights. Bikes cost AU$30 per day and come with helmets.

Manly Bike Tours

6/54 West Esplanade, Manly
(entrance off Belgrave Street)
Tel: 02 8005 7368
www.manlybiketours.com.au
Open: daily, 9am–6pm

As well as the main promenade, Manly has a stack of smaller beaches and a national park to explore. All kinds of bikes are available to hire including two-seater tandem cruisers, and detailed maps featuring local secrets are handed out with each rental. Directionless cyclists may want to join the tour instead to be guided by the experts – they meet every morning at 10.30am outside the shop.

GOLF

The Coast Golf & Recreation Club

1430 Anzac Parade, Little Bay
Tel: 02 9311 7422
www.coastgolf.com.au

Spectacular ocean views, rolling contours and blind shots aplenty, 'The Coastie' has 18 championship holes spread out across a challenging coastal terrain. It's as close to Scotland as you can get, but it's in a fairly remote end of Sydney and you may have a fair wait for a taxi.

Long Reef Golf Club

Anzac Avenue, Collaroy
Tel: 02 9971 8113
www.longreefgolfclub.com.au

play...

The Links at Long Reef is a brilliant public 18-hole course with sweeping, challenging fairways. It's set along the coastline (though protected from the wind) with a beautiful view across the northern beaches. The oceanfront clubhouse is worth a few (dozen) drinks, too.

NSW Golf Club

Henry Head, Botany Bay National Park, La Perouse
Tel: 02 9661 4455
www.nswgolfclub.com.au

You may struggle to keep an eye on the ball – the ocean views from this A-class course are that magnificent. Though it can cop a buffeting from the wind, this course is rated as one of the top 50 short courses in the world – Golf Digest ranks it fairly highly among clubs outside the UK and USA. It's a private club, though non-members can make booking on weekdays, but you need to get in early – it fills up quickly.

Woollahra Golf Club

O'Sullivan Road, Bellevue Hill
Tel: 02 9327 5404
www.woollahragolfclub.com

Close to the city, the club's nine (perfectly manicured) holes are challenging enough for intermediate players – check the website for various public sessions. Though it's leafy and well maintained, it does get crowded.

HEIGHTS

Bridge Climb

3 Cumberland Street, The Rocks
Tel: 02 8274 7777
www.bridgeclimb.com

For vertigo-inducing views over Sydney and a once-in-a-lifetime thrill, conquer what Aussies call 'The Coathanger' on a giddying three-hour guided climb to the top of the Harbour Bridge. The tours take groups of 14 people during the day, night, twilight and at the break of dawn with prices ranging from AU$198–298 per person. Be warned; every climber must endure the indignity of a one-piece jumpsuit.

Seaplane

Woollahra Sailing Club, 1 Vickery Avenue, Rose Bay
Tel: 02 9388 1978
www.seaplanes.com.au

Sydney looks sexy from the ground, but from the air she's a goddess. Scenic flights take in the best of the city's harbours, beaches and sights from the harbour to Manly and all the way up to the iconic Palm Beach peninsula – where Australia's favourite soap, Home & Away, is filmed. If you want to skip pesky traffic and arrive like a rock star, the company arranges fly-and-dine deals – ideal if you're lunching at Jonah's in Whale Beach. Flights start at AU$175 per person.

KAYAKING

Oz Paddle
Various venues around Sydney: Balmoral
Beach, Rose Bay and Woolloomooloo
www.ozpaddle.com.au
Open: daily from 8am

Who needs a boat when you can
sightsee and tone your triceps at the
same time? This company rents out a
range of single and double crafts from
AU$20 an hour, launching from vari-
ous points around Sydney. The peaceful harbour around Balmoral boasts
idyllic coves – you can even kayak to
other beaches like Chinamans. If you
launch at Rose Bay, you can paddle
out to Shark Island. It also offers tours
for two-three hours exploring Sydney
harbour for AU$90 per person. Re-
member to bring something to swim in
and slap on the high-factor sunscreen.

PARKS & GARDENS

Centennial Park
Tel: 02 9339 6699
www.centennialparklands.com.au
Open: daily, sunrise to sunset
Visitor information centre: daily, 9am–
4pm Mon–Fri; 10am–3pm Sat/Sun

Whether you want an uninterrupted
3.8-kilometre running and cycling
track, playing fields or picnic and BBQ
facilities, the 189-hectare Centennial
Park has the space. In the middle of
the Eastern Suburbs, these sprawling gardens are an oasis of tranquil-
lity, with tall Port Jackson figs and oak
trees, lakes filled with ducks and swans,

beautiful rose gardens, wetlands and
swamp walks. There's even horse riding available at the Centennial Parklands Equestrian Centre. If you visit in
summer, check out Moonlight Cinema,
an outdoor cinema festival where you
can watch films al fresco on beanbags,
from December to March.

Royal Botanic Gardens
Mrs Macquaries Road, Sydney
Tel: 02 9231 8111
www.rbgsyd.nsw.gov.au
Admission is free but entrance to the
Tropical Centre costs around AU$3.30

It's hard to believe this stunning
30-hectare garden was basically a veg-
gie patch for Governor Phillip some
200 years ago. Today, the gardens boast
more than one-million plant species.
Walking through the gnarled 200-year-
old fig trees, ancient Wollemi Pines and
flower gardens as hundreds of fruit bats
screech is a delight. Plus, there are uninterrupted harbour views and endless
manicured grass for picnicking. Make a
day of it by starting at the Art Gallery
of NSW (see Culture), strolling through
the rolling lawns of The Domain
(where Sydney holds a stack of free
outdoor film and music festivals during
summer) and ambling along the foreshore to Lady Macquarie's Chair, the
site of the St. George OpenAir cinema
festival in summer. Films are projected
on a massive screen that rises from
the harbour at nightfall. Be quick if
you want tickets – there are only 1,800
seats and they sell out fast.

play...

Rushcutters Bay Park

Corner of New South Head Road and
New Beach Road, Rushcutters Bay

Awash with personal trainers, joggers, picnicking groups and mums with prams, Rushcutters Bay Park is a favourite for Eastern Suburbs residents – it's an easy five-minute walk from Potts Point and Kings Cross. There's plenty of shade with leafy native trees packed with kookaburras and fruit bats, and the view isn't bad, either – it straddles a bay filled with gleaming white yachts berthed at the CYC Sailing Club, with plenty of grass, playing fields, playgrounds and pathways popular with joggers. Take a picnic rug and spend the day horizontal or pull up a plastic chair at the kiosk, which does a roaring trade in coffee, sandwiches and salads.

SCUBA DIVING

Dive Sydney

10 Belgrave Street, Manly
Tel: 02 9977 4355
www.divesydney.com.au
Open: daily, 9am (8am Sat/Sun)–6pm
(8pm Thurs)

This PADI 5-Star Instructor training facility offers all courses from beginner to pro, with a brand spanking new dive training pool, classrooms and attached retail store. Its shore dives concentrate around Manly, such as Shelly Beach and Fairy Bower reef. Boat dives depart from the Manly headquarters every Friday, Saturday and Sunday at 9am, 11am and 1pm.

Pro Dive

169 Pittwater Road, Manly
Tel: 02 9977 5966
www.prodivesydney.com
Open: daily, 10am (9am Thurs/Fri, 8am
Sat/Sun)–5pm (7pm Thurs, 6pm
Fri–Sun)

Pro Dive runs everything from Open Water to more advanced courses in two sites: Manly and Coogee (27 Alfreda Street, tel: 02 9315 8149). It offers a free mini-bus pick-up from Pitt Street if you're diving in Manly, and various pick-up points if you're diving in Coogee. Its custom-designed dive boat, Sealife V, departs from Rose Bay Ferry Wharf and Manly Yacht club. Night dives are scheduled on Thursdays.

SPAS

Amy Erbacher Beauty

4 New Mclean Street, Edgecliff
Tel: 04 2322 2422
www.amyerbacher.com.au
Open: by appointment only

After years of being on camera, former model and television presenter Amy Erbacher learned a thing or two about beauty, so she swapped her glamorous career to study beauty and pursue her passion for effective, individually customised skincare. From facials, manicures and pedicures to waxing and body treatments, Amy is an effervescent host, fussing over her clients in her private residence with the kind of attentiveness and personable care other day spas couldn't possibly replicate. She uses Payot, an array of organic products and cosmeceutical vitamin boosters such as A, C, Beta-Glucan

Open: daily, 6am (6.30am Sat/Sun)–6.30pm
Entry: AU$5

A Bondi institution, this 50-metre ocean pool doesn't have to try hard to look enticing – it sits astride the rolling waves of south Bondi Beach, beneath Icebergs, one of Sydney's most glam restaurants and cocktail bars. The baths were originally created back in 1929 to encourage local lifesavers to keep up their fitness during the winter months. There are eight lanes, a sauna, a gym and yoga classes, and while temperatures are at the mercy of the ocean currents, spare a thought for the Bondi Icebergs club swimmers. In winter, they make a show of dropping huge slabs of ice into the pool, diving in to swim in teeth-chatteringly cold water.

McIvers Baths is a rock pool about 50 metres north of Wylie's Baths. It's a slip of a pool – only about 20-metres long with natural rock walls and waves rolling gently over the sea wall, yet it's loved for its serene, female-only atmosphere. Few Sydney women know this little gem, but its well-known to Muslim women, nuns, lesbians and simply those who are tired of pervy men on Sydney beaches. The facilities are very basic, with cold showers and a few grassed areas to sunbathe on, but the uninterrupted ocean view is magnificent. The entry fee is strictly for upkeep and not profit, meaning you only need to part with a mere 20 cents per visit (if there's no one stationed in the spartan clubhouse, be honest and throw your coins in the ice-cream tub through the gate).

McIvers Baths
Beach Street (through Grant Reserve Park), South Coogee
www.randwick.nsw.gov.au
Open: daily, 7am–5pm
Entry: AU$0.20

North Sydney Pool
4 Alfred Street South, North Sydney
Tel: 02 9955 2309
www.northsydney.nsw.gov.au
Open: daily, 5.30am–9pm Mon–Fri;
7am–7pm Sat/Sun
Entry: AU$6.50

play...

Its million-dollar location is the icing on the cake for this outdoor Olympic-sized swimming pool. Positioned below the north side of the Sydney Harbour Bridge, these nine-lanes are home ground to many Olympic athletes and though the grandstand to one side and limited decked area doesn't offer a huge amount of poolside lazing potential, the location, and the chance to swim 100 metres without turning, makes it a firm favourite for serious freestylers.

Wylie's Baths *(right)*
Neptune Street (corner of Beach Street),
South Coogee
Tel: 02 9665 2838
www.wylies.com.au
Open: daily, 7am–5pm (7pm summer)

If you're not in the mood for sand but still want to splash around in salty water, an ocean pool is the next best thing. This one is one of Sydney's best, situated just underneath the cliffs at South Coogee, a short walk from Coogee Beach. Named after Henry Alexander Wylie, a champion long-distance swimmer, Wylie's has a 50-metre outdoor tidal pool with a natural rock base, just alongside the crashing surf, with incredible views to Coogee Beach and out to Wedding Cake Island. There's a decked area for sun-soaking, a kiosk for casual snacks and coffee, regular outdoor yoga classes, and you can even have an outdoor massage on the decked area upstairs.

WALKS

Bondi to Bronte
From Notts Avenue, Bondi
to Arden Street, Coogee

If it's a blisteringly beautiful Sydney day, the views will bring a tear to your eye, so tag this coastal walk as one of those Sydney must-dos. It takes in dramatic cliffs, stunning beaches and bays along the way and is around 4.5 kilometres return – but expect to jostle for space with the fitness junkies jogging along the path.

The Federation Cliff Walk
From Raleigh Reserve in Dover Heights
to Watsons Bay

With a tremendous vista of the wild Tasman Sea, this two-hour, three-kilometre walk starts at Dover Heights where it winds along boardwalks built along precipitous sandstone bluffs. It then passes the tranquil, harbour-facing Camp Cove beach and finishes at Watsons Bay, where you can refuel with fish and chips before catching a ferry back to Circular Quay.

Hermitage Walk
Start at Dumaresq Reserve in Rose
Bay, head up New South Head Road,
left into Tivoli Avenue, left into Bay
View Hill Road and follow the signs

The views along this 1.4-kilometre walking track take in million-dollar yachts, the Sydney Harbour Bridge and the Opera House, passing petite coves and lesser-known harbour beaches like

Milk Beach. Finish at the gorgeous harbour beach Nielsen Park, where you can stop for a swim, have lunch at the café and catch a bus back to the city.

Taronga to Balmoral
Take the ferry from Circular Quay to Taronga Wharf

This walk winds through bush tracks along the coast and takes under two hours, with stupendous views across Sydney harbour and out to the headlands. Start at Taronga Zoo Wharf then head through native bushland of Bradleys Head to the peaceful beach at Clifton Gardens and Chowder Bay, where you can stop for a coffee or lunch. Continue on to Balmoral Beach and catch the 238 bus back to Taronga Wharf.

play...

info...

Dangers

The biggest danger to the average tourist is underestimating the surf and powerful rip currents (undertows) at Sydney's beaches, which sadly cause all too many drowning tragedies each year. Bondi's lifeguards and lifesavers rescue around 2,500 people per year – and 85 per cent of these rescues are tourists. There's even a permanent Bondi rip current dubbed 'The Backpacker Express'. Ocean beaches are generally patrolled by surf lifesavers during the busy summer months, and even if you consider yourself an experienced swimmer, it's crucial to swim between the safest area marked by red and yellow flags posted on the sand. If you run into any trouble or get caught in a rip, don't panic or try to swim against the current – swim parallel to the shore, or simply raise your hand and wave at the lifesavers for help. For more information about surf conditions and advice, visit www.surflifesavingsydney.com.au. Another danger is Australia's powerful sun, best avoided between 11am and 2pm. Locals have grown up with the slip-slop-slap mantra (slip on a t-shirt, slop on some sunscreen, slap on a hat) – follow their lead, or end up a fetching shade of lobster red.

Dressing

Lackadaisical locals have the casual, relaxed look down to an art form – jeans, shorts and thongs (flip-flops – not the skimpy underwear, though Lord knows what lurks beneath skimpy clothing) are worn everywhere, even in the centre of the CBD. At Manly and Bondi, it's normal to see shirtless men and women wearing a bikini top and cut-off denim shorts on the street or in cafés. During the evening, Sydneysiders make more of an effort – well, most do – and unless you're spending the night at a pub, it's better to play it safe and follow suit. Most upmarket bars and nightclubs enforce a dress code for general entry, such as no thongs, shorts or sleeveless tops. Glam-up or go home, in other words.

Money

The cost of living la vida Sydney usually surprises visitors. Prices have increased quite noticeably over the past few years – be prepared to pay upwards of AU$3 for a coffee, AU$4-6 for a schooner of beer and between AU$16-20 for a cocktail. Withdraw your cash from any one of the bank ATMs, which are located all over the city and within some convenience stores and petrol stations. Credit cards are accepted everywhere – it's also commonplace to 'run a tab' at bars and pubs, leaving your credit card behind the bar as you drink. Everything you consume is tallied up as you go, and settled when you leave.

Opening hours & Public Holidays

Opening Hours: Businesses, banks and retailers are generally open Monday to Friday from 9am to 5pm, give or take an hour or two. Shopping malls and most boutiques are open on weekends, with 24-hour convenience stores and petrol stations scattered around the city. Many bars tend to close on Mondays after the busy weekend rush.

Public holidays: Aussies consider these their birth right, and in addition to Good Friday, Easter Saturday and Easter Monday, Christmas and New Year's Day, Australia's work-free days are as follows:

Australia Day - 26th January
Boxing Day - first weekday after Christmas
Anzac Day - 25th April
Queen's Birthday - 1st Monday in June
Labour Day - 1st Monday in October
Bank Holiday - 1st Monday in August

In NSW, public holidays usually mean restricted operating hours for businesses and transport services, though most shopping malls operate seven days, with extended hours for die-hard shoppers. The bad news? Prices for accommodation and flights are increased. The good news? Many of the best music festivals take place during these long weekends, and if a public holiday falls on a weekend, it's carried over to a weekday. Aussies wouldn't have it any other way.

Public Transport

Navigating Sydney by public transport isn't particularly efficient when compared to the comprehensive network of systems in London, New York or Paris, but the city's buses offer various routes throughout the city to areas like Paddington, Bondi and Surry Hills. Look out for the Sydney Explorer and Bondi Explorer, which offer convenient hop-on, hop-off sightseeing tours to all the major tourist spots (see www.sydneyexplorer.info). Travelling by train isn't exactly convenient, however. Visitors mostly use the City Circle Line, which stops at the city's major precincts like Circular Quay, Wynyard, Town Hall, Central, Museum and St. James and Martin Place. Ferries (www.sydneyferries.info) are a scenic way to take in Sydney Harbour and explore beautiful harbours and the beach areas of Manly, Watsons Bay and Rose Bay – the main terminal is located at Circular Quay. For a full range of transport options visit the Sydney Transport Infoline at www.131500.info.

Taxis

Taxis are clearly marked and numerous companies cruise the streets including Taxis Combined (133 300), Premier Cabs (13 10 17) and ABC cabs (13 25 22). For a little leather-seat luxury, hail a Silver Service cab (133 100). Vacant cabs illuminate their rooftop light – hail one simply by sticking your hand out or waving; most will pull over wherever they can do so safely. There are designated taxi ranks scattered throughout the city; on George Street near The Rocks, on the corner of Park Street near McDonald's, outside Central Station on Elizabeth Street, outside the David Jones department store on Market Street and at World Square on George Street between Liverpool Street and Goulburn Street. In Kings Cross there is a secure taxi rank on Bayswater Road. There's no need to worry about the fare as all taxis use meters. Fares start at AU$3.30 from 10am (an additional 20 per cent surcharge is added from 6pm) and are calculated at AU$1.99 per kilometre – passengers must also pay any road or bridge tolls. Annoyingly, many cabbies are notorious for being difficult around their shift change-over time at 3am. Even though it's illegal, many will stop at the kerb and ask where you are going – charging off without so much as a 'so long, suckers' if your destination doesn't suit them. It's maddening, to say the least, and worth keeping in mind if you're planning a night out.

Tipping

Though not mandatory, tipping is widely practised at Sydney's upmarket restaurants and bars. A small token of appreciation will be warmly received by hardworking cocktail bartenders and waitstaff who take their craft very seriously. Ten per cent is about right – more if you're feeling generous.

Weather

No surprises that the best time to visit Sydney is during the warmer months between October to April, though the visions you had of lazy summer days lounging at the beach can evaporate in a flash – Sydney summers are notoriously unstable; think thunderstorms and torrential downpours one day and near-perfect 35-degree, blue-sky days the next. Winter months are fairly mild – on a good day it's possible to sit in a T-shirt and have a dip in the ocean, though temperatures can become chilly.

index...

Hedonism /hedoniz'm/

'The philosophy that pleasure is the highest
good and proper aim of human life.'

– Oxford English Dictionary

Hg2 Corporate

Branded Gifts....

Looking for a corporate gift with real value? Want to reinforce your company's presence at a conference or event? We can provide you with branded guides so recipients will explore their chosen city with your company's logo right under their nose.

Branding can go from a small logo discreetly embossed on to our standard cover, to a fully custom jacket in your company's colours and in a material of your choice. We can also include a letter from your CEO/Chairman/President and add or remove as much or as little other content as you require. We can create a smaller, 'best of' guide, branded with your company's livery in a format of your choice. Custom guides can also be researched and created from scratch to any destination not yet on our list.

For more information, please contact Tremayne at tremayne@hg2.com

Content licensing....

We can also populate your own website or other materials with our in-depth content, superb imagery and insider knowledge.

For more information, please contact Tremayne at tremayne@hg2.com

Hg-Who?

Welcome to the world of Hg2 – the UK's leading luxury city guide series. Launched in 2004 as the *A Hedonist's guide to…* series, we are pleased to announce a new look to our guides, now called simply Hg2. In response to customer feedback, the new Hg2 is 25% lighter, even more luxurious to look at or touch, and flexible, for greater portability. However, fear not, our content is still as meticulously researched and well-illustrated as ever and the spirit of hedonism still infuses our work. Our brand of hedonism taps into the spirit of 'Whatever Works for You' – from chic boutique hotels to well-kept-secret restaurants, to the very best cup of coffee in town. We do not mindlessly seek out the most expensive; instead, we search high and low for the very best each city has to offer.

So take Hg2 as your companion to a city. Written by well-regarded journalists and constantly updated online at www.Hg2.com (register this guide to get one year of free access), it will help you Sleep, Eat, Drink, Shop, Party and Play like a sophisticated local.

"Hg2 is about foreign life as art" **Vanity Fair**
"The new travel must-haves" **Daily Telegraph**
"Insight into what's really going on" **Tatler**
"A minor bible" **New York Times**
"Excellent guides for stylish travellers" **Harper's Bazaar**
"Discerning travellers, rejoice!" **Condé Nast Traveller**